HATE SPEECH, SEX SPEECH, FREE SPEECH

HATE SPEECH, SEX SPEECH, FREE SPEECH

Nicholas Wolfson

PRAEGER

Westport, Connecticut
London

KF
4772
.W65
1997

Library of Congress Cataloging-in-Publication Data

Wolfson, Nicholas.
    Hate speech, sex speech, free speech / Nicholas Wolfson.
      p. cm.
    Includes bibliographical references and index.
    ISBN 0–275–95770–5 (alk. paper)
      1. Freedom of speech—United States. 2. Hate speech—United
States. 3. Pornography—United States. 4. Sexual harassment—Law
and legislation—United States. 5. Racism in language. I. Title.
    KF4772.W65   1997
    342.73'0853—dc20
    [347.302853]   96–44680

British Library Cataloguing in Publication Data is available.

Library of Congress Catalog Card Number: 96–44680
ISBN: 0–275–95770–5

First published in 1997

Praeger Publishers, 88 Post Road West, Westport, CT 06881
An imprint of Greenwood Publishing Group, Inc.

Printed in the United States of America

∞™

The paper used in this book complies with the
Permanent Paper Standard issued by the National
Information Standards Organization (Z39.48–1984).

10 9 8 7 6 5 4 3 2

Copyright Acknowledgments

The author and publisher are grateful for permission to reprint material from the following copyrighted sources:

Wolfson, Nicholas, *Free Speech Theory and Hateful Words*, 60 University of Cincinnati Law Review 1 (1991). Reprinted by permission of the copyright holder, University of Cincinnati Law Review.

Wolfson, Nicholas, *Equality in First Amendment Theory*, 38 St. Louis University Law Journal 379 (1993–1994). Reprinted by permission of the copyright holder, St. Louis University Law Journal.

Wolfson, Nicholas, *Eroticism, Obscenity, Pornography and Free Speech*, 60 Brooklyn Law Review 1037 (1994). Reprinted by permission of the copyright holder, Brooklyn Law Review.

*To my beloved wife, Judith,
who makes everything possible*

.

CONTENTS

CHAPTER 1

INTRODUCTION

The traditional, liberal, civil rights position on free speech issues is under powerful assault in the academy. Old allies in the liberal alliance have parted company. Feminist and African-American intellectuals, as well as many white male scholars, now question the old notion that strong free-speech protection is not only defensible but offers the best route to a just society. Rather, the new critics of the old liberal verities argue on a number of fronts that the strong version of free speech disenfranchises blacks, women, gays, and lesbians.

Two kinds of speech are singled out. First, there is hate speech. It is difficult to define this category precisely, but it generally includes offensive speech directed at minorities. In its most vulgar form, it includes the racial and sexist epithet, such as "kike" and "fag." At a more subtle level, or so it is argued, it includes books, cinema, and television images that demean a minority. For example, many African-Americans view the American classic *The Adventures of Huckleberry Finn* as an example of hate speech. (Some Jews view portions of the New Testament as hate speech directed at Jews, the alleged killers of God; although no one argues for its censorship, many call for clarification.)

Hate speech is criticized as lacking any of the elements that

warrant constitutional protection. Hence, scores of universities have enacted speech codes that ban hate speech. It is
depicted as emotional speech without intellectual content.
Worse, the new critics of the First Amendment argue that hate
speech is false, lacking any basis in science or enlightened culture. Worst of all, such speech degrades the objects of abuse,
silences them through fear, does them psychological damage,
and creates a smarmy and nauseating culture that harms
women and minorities.

Another criticized category of speech (and image) is pornography. Modern feminist scholars have eloquently argued
that pornography is a zero-value form of expression that
maintains patriarchal dominion over women in Western (and
in fact all) cultures. Indeed, they argue, it is not expression at
all but an act of violence against women that silences and
harms them. Even pornographic art, cinema, or television that
reflects talent or even genius is so harmful that it should be
censored.

The eloquent criticisms of hate speech and pornography are
based in large measure on alleged disparities in speech power
between women and minorities on one hand, and white males
in the modern age of corporate giants and billionaire entrepreneurs on the other. Constitutional scholars have begun to
pay attention to the problem of speech inequality. While traditional civil libertarians continue to find their inspiration in
the nearly absolute language of the First Amendment, other
scholars are increasingly looking to the equality language of
the Fourteenth Amendment or to general principles of egalitarianism.[1]

Feminist theorists argue that American society is so inherently sexist that, as we have indicated above, the constitutional protection of speech actually serves to subordinate
women.[2] Two frequently cited examples of speech-as-
subordinator are pornography[3] and verbal sexual harassment
in the workplace, such as festooning shops or offices with

photographs of women in sexually provocative poses.[4] Feminists consider these to be methods of warfare by men against women, because they treat women as sexual objects, reflecting both the subordinate position of women and the preservation of male dominance. Many view these activities as political speech inherent in the war of the sexes, in which women are often the losers.

In this view, sexist talk is a weapon used by men in a ceaseless gender war. Sexist talk is a deeply structured and fundamental, albeit perverse, means by which men define their status and, indeed, their meaning. As Nancy S. Ehrenreich put it, "Under this view, [a female worker's] insistence that [a male worker] refrain from displaying pornography would have prevented him from following a fundamental tenet of his group's philosophy and undermined the sense of identity, of maleness, that the act of displaying pornography affirms."[5] Limiting his freedom would assist women's political battle for power but necessarily limit his power and that of the male class.

Feminists argue that pornography and sexually harassing words in the workplace enforce men's dominance and efforts to subordinate women. As Kathryn Abrams eloquently argues, "Pornography on an employer's wall or desk communicates a message about the way he views women, a view strikingly at odds with the way women wish to be viewed in the workplace. . . . It may communicate that women should be the objects of sexual aggression, that they are submissive slaves to male desires."[6]

Abrams refers to empirical investigations indicating that "women are more likely to regard a sexual encounter, *verbal* or physical, as coercive."[7] She further asserts that "men are less likely to regard such conduct as harassing, and more likely to view it as a flattering reflection on their physical or personal attributes."[8] She concludes that male judges may reach results that do not chill "verbal sexual abuse . . . and dissemination or display of pornography."[9] To the argument that courts should adopt an attitude that "reflects both men's and women's views of sexually oriented conduct in the workplace," Abrams responds that equal perspectives will perpetuate the subordination of women.[10]

Minority rights theoreticians also make this inequality argument with great vigor. Constitutional law scholars have written in recent years about the alleged inability of African-Americans, Hispanics, gays, and lesbians to engage effectively in the so-called "free market of ideas" because of the imbalance of power inherent in a racist society.[11] Hence, many colleges and universities have enacted speech codes that attempt to redress the imbalance by banning offensive racist, sexist, and homophobic speech.[12]

Any effort to ration speech, however, carries with it extremely serious consequences. In the first place, there are some obvious problems. Who is to ration? How can we trust the rationers? The risk of bias is enormous. Politicians and bureaucrats cannot be trusted to allocate speech to people or causes they dislike. Conflicts of interest arise. Government officials are not likely to apportion "speech chits" to individuals who may expose government peccadillos. The dominant political forces of the moment will seldom allocate speech in a manner that will threaten them.

How could we ration? What standards could we use? African-Americans, for example, might demand that 12 percent of every opinion section of a newspaper be devoted to African-American causes. Hispanics might demand a quota based upon their own percentage of the population; religious fundamentalists might make a similar demand; and feminists might demand a percentage devoted to their causes. Affirmative action and quotas would radically alter the essence of speech and the speech dialectic. Speech is dynamic; it moves and convinces in mysterious and unpredictable ways. Speech is the essential attribute of humanity, close to the core of human autonomy. A cabining and leveling of speech might reduce and diminish the human spirit.

Nevertheless, certain feminist and minority spokespersons fear failure of their cause without a sort of affirmative action for "proper speech" and limits on speech that allegedly drowns out feminist and minority voices (even though their ideas have triumphed in key establishments). A remarkable *New York Times* article by Alessandra Stanley describes the almost absolute dominion of liberal political voices in Hollywood.[13] She reports how directors and actors with conservative viewpoints must hide their opinions or risk almost certain industry retribution.[14] The same, as many assert, is often true in our prestigious universities.[15]

Feminist and minority speech has had a dramatic effect on American mores. The intellectual redoubts—elite universities, the media, and the cinema—are clearly in the hands of liberal and left-wing men and women. On the other hand, religious and political conservatives are outraged at the imbalance in favor of liberal and radical visions of economics, gender, and race in cinema, television, and the university.[16]

Through novels, cinema, television, and scholarly research, free speech in the capitalistic West has transformed the societal vision of women's roles. Men in the workplace, blue collar and white, have begun to internalize a proper vision of women, racial minorities, gays, and lesbians. Free speech, as currently defined, has been a weapon for feminism, and for gay and lesbian rights. Subjugated groups will restrict it only at great cost. Restrictions may create resentment and anger; they may prolong the battle for equality rather than shorten it.

Of course, women, racial minorities, and the gay and lesbian communities are impatient with the pace of progress. Some believe that the 1992 Republican presidential convention demonstrated the power of feminist, gay, and lesbian-bashing. The 1994 Republican sweep aroused great fear in liberal groups. (On the other hand, it has encouraged conservative groups who fear the liberal "bias" of the media and Hollywood). But these sentiments do not necessarily militate for censorship. The world is surfeit with examples of groups impatient with the progress of certain ideas and the possibility of rapid peaceful change who sought victory not by speech but by censoring it. History teaches that unacceptable levels of government coercion and force lie in that direction.

But this view of progress may be Panglossian. There are no guarantees that speech we despise will fail. The cruel dilemma is that left unfettered, certain ideas triumph, and some perspectives will see them as bad ones. Speech is fluid. It moves with an unpredictable dynamic and is inherently incompatible with balance. Ideas are born, develop, and dominate, or languish and perish, as part of a complex interaction of culture and dialectic that cannot be easily described or reduced to a cookbook formula. Speech rationing would attempt something like a fix or stasis in the dialectic based upon a belief in a "just" balance. The fix would be governed by a belief in a "rational" and "truthful" end or goal for society. Given the unpredictable and sometimes dangerous dynamic of speech, the issue is then the following: Why should we permit hateful or sexually offensive speech?

In this book we attempt to answer this question. In Chapter 2 we advance a skeptical, pragmatic basis for a strong version of the First Amendment, one that protects the most offensive forms of speech, including hate speech. We point out that in areas as diverse as physics, politics, and art, the truth is ascertained by a process of debate and conversation. The process is risky and unpredictable and, therefore, instructive. The human conversation as a path toward knowledge can never end, because, although God is infallible and knows the Truth, we are not and do not. Indeed, even those among us with religious faith should not wish to end the dialogue, because we see as through a glass darkly and can profit from argument. Thus, there are powerful religious arguments for a tolerant, pragmatic approach to free speech. We point out that efforts to censor offensive speech as untrue rest upon the dangerous premise that courts can distinguish between genuine areas of controversy and subjects in which the search for verity has ended.

In Chapter 3 we pursue the hate speech controversy and argue that censorship of hate speech will have dangerous consequences for the concept of free speech. We find that efforts to censor hateful thoughts, unless limited to the four-letter word, may lead to censorship of a great swath of learned and sacred works. In Chapter 4 we concentrate on the arguments that speech of the disadvantaged must be subsidized and speech of the powerful chilled, endeavoring to demonstrate how pervasive thought control will ensue from such an approach. We point out the difficulty of determining what groups are subjugated; for example, conservatives claim that the media is tilted against them, and religious conservatives argue that the movie and television industries do not give them an even break. Liberals read the matter differently. In Chapter 5 we criticize efforts to censor pornography and obscenity. We argue that courts and certain interest groups fear the language and images of sex because they involve issues that are, in their opinion, more significant and dangerous politically than dull stuff about tariffs, taxes, and the minimum wage.

NOTES

1. *See e.g.*, Charles R. Lawrence, *If He Hollers Let Him Go: Regulating Racist Speech On Campus*, 1990 Duke L. J. 431, 438–49 (1990) (*Brown v. Board of Education* justifies regulation of hate

speech); Mari J. Matsuda, *Public Response to Racist Speech: Considering the Victim's Story*, 87 Mich. L. Rev. 2320, 2377 (1989) (Bill of Rights' central principle is that all are "entitled to basic dignity, to nondiscrimination and to the freedom to participate fully in society"); Catharine A. MacKinnon, *Pornography, Civil Rights, and Speech*, 20 Harv. C.R.-C.L. L. Rev. 1 (1985) (describing pornography as a civil rights violation); Cass R. Sunstein, *Free Speech Now*, 59 U. Chi. L. Rev. 255 (1992) (approving of government action to diversify content of speech and arguing that speech protection should focus on political discourse).

2. *See* Mary E. Becker, *The Politics of Women's Wrongs and the Bill of "Rights": A Bicentennial Perspective*, 59 U. Chi. L. Rev. 453, 486–94 (1992).

3. *See* Andrea Dworkin & Catharine A. MacKinnon, *Pornography and Civil Rights: A New Day for Women's Equality* 139–41 (1988) (proposing an anti-pornography ordinance).

4. *See* Nancy S. Ehrenreich, *Pluralist Myths and Powerful Men: The Ideology of Reasonableness in Sexual Harassment Law*, 99 Yale L.J. 1177 (1990); Susan Estrich, *Sex at Work*, 43 Stan. L. Rev. 813 (1991); Kathryn Abrams, *Gender Discrimination and the Transformation of Workplace Norms*, 42 Vand. L. Rev. 1183 (1989); Marcy Strauss, *Sexual Speech in the Workplace*, 25 Harv. C.R.-C.L. L. Rev. 1 (1990); *see also* Harris v. Forklift, 114 S. Ct. 367 (1993).

5. Ehrenreich, *supra* note 4, at 1222.

6. Abrams, *supra* note 4, at 1212 n. 118.

7. *Id.* at 1206 (emphasis added).

8. *Id.* at 1206.

9. *Id.*

10. *Id.* at 1207 n. 103.

11. *See, e.g.*, Richard Delgado, *Campus Antiracism Rules: Constitutional Narratives in Collision*, 85 Nw. U.L. Rev. 343 (1991); Lawrence, *supra* note 1; Matsuda, *supra* note 1.

12. *See* Nat Hentoff, *"Speech Codes" on the Campus and Problems of Free Speech, in* Debating P. C. 215 (Paul Berman, ed., 1992). Nat Hentoff cites, among others, an example from Stanford where minority groups called for speech codes. One student leader said, "We don't put as many restrictions on freedom of speech as we should."

Id. at 216. Hentoff commented that such leaders "have learned . . . that censorship is okay provided your motives are okay." *Id.*

13. Alessandra Stanley, *Hidden Hollywood*, N.Y. Times, May 31, 1992, § 9, at 1.

14. *Id.*

15. *See, e.g.*, Dinesh D'Souza, *Illiberal Education: The Politics of Race and Sex on Campus* (1991).

16. *See, e.g.*, Richard J. Neuhaus, *The Naked Public Square: Religion and Democracy in America* (1984).

CHAPTER 2

PRAGMATISM AND WORDS THAT HURT

In a homogenous and closed society there are certain moral absolutes that none question. As Thomas Pangle put it, "Plato and Aristotle were convinced that all societies—even, or especially healthy republics—are necessarily closed. Every society will have certain fundamental sanctities or moral absolutes whose doubt is truly upsetting to that society, and that a responsible philosopher will in public treat with the greatest caution."[1]

In such a society, voluntary and virtually unanimous agreement on core principles can guide speech censors. But as Pangle points out, quoting Spinoza, we live in a society where "every man may think as he pleases, and say what he thinks."[2] We live in a diverse, relativistic, cynical, fractious, divided, and contentious society, one with bitter cultural divisions over sex, family, values, and fundamental goals of life.

There is a danger in facilitating debate about explosive core issues.[3] As Socrates said:

> We have convictions [perhaps fewer of us in today's world] from our childhood about just and noble things, convictions under which we were brought up . . . and then there are other practices opposed to these convic-

tions, practices that bring pleasure, and that flatter one's soul and draw it to them. They do not persuade those who are at all men of measure . . . but when to someone so disposed, the question is put: "What is noble?"—and, when he answers what he heard from the lawgiver, the rational argument refutes him, and this refutation is repeated often, and in many ways, he falls into the opinion that nothing is any more noble than base; and the same happens regarding the just and the good and the matters he especially held in honor.[4]

We no longer live in the relatively confident world of the classic Greek age. We do not live with the unified belief system of twelfth, thirteenth, or fourteenth-century Europe, where intellectuals and the masses believed in the religious bases of morality and politics. In the age of the Enlightenment, European intellectuals replaced religion with "pure" reason and expected that reason would provide the unifying and transcendental moral and political foundations for the just society.[5] Yet in our postmodern world, political and intellectual leaders no longer believe in the unifying power of pure reason.[6] Reason is seen as imbedded in culture and contingency. Truth is not "out there,"[7] ready to be discovered by religion, philosophy, law, or political science. As the pragmatist philosopher Richard Rorty points out, truth is what we reach in the process of debate and consensus.

About two hundred years ago, the idea that truth was made rather than found began to take hold of the imagination of Europe. The French Revolution had shown that the whole vocabulary of social relations, and the whole spectrum of social institutions, could be replaced almost overnight. . . .

At about the same time, the Romantic poets were showing what happens when art is thought of no longer as imitation, but, rather, as the artist's self-creation.[8]

Not even science escapes pragmatic interpretation. Science does not find hard "facts," independent of theory and debate and existing forever.[9] Newton's "truth" was replaced by quantum theory and relativity, and new "truths" may emerge as a result of further investigation and debate in the scientific community.

Today's diverse, argumentative, liberal society is based upon a non-absolutist, non-universalist worldview. Rorty quotes Joseph Schumpeter to argue that an individual must "realize the relative validity of one's convictions and yet stand for them unflinchingly; [this is what] distinguishes a civilized man from a barbarian."[10] As Isaiah Berlin states, "To demand more than this is perhaps a deep and incurable metaphysical need; but to allow it to determine one's practice is a symptom of an equally deep, and more dangerous, moral and political immaturity."[11] In fact, it is that pragmatic lack of metaphysical belief in truths that characterizes a free society. As Richard Rorty puts it, "It is central to the idea of a liberal society that in respect to words as opposed to deeds, persuasion as opposed to force, anything goes. This openmindedness should not be fostered because as Scripture teaches, Truth is great and will prevail, nor because, as Milton suggests, Truth will always win in a free and open encounter. It should be fostered for its own sake. *A liberal society is one which is content to call 'true' whatever the upshot of such encounters turns out to be.*"[12]

The constitutional doctrine of free speech in considerable measure presupposes this pragmatic approach to truth. Under First Amendment theory, "anything goes" in political speech, subject to such exceptions as fighting words and defamation. If truth is out there to be found, if speech is a method of describing a reality that all will recognize, then perhaps free speech must be severely limited; debate, discussion, and political theory will ultimately reach the truth, and at that point it is absurd to permit further debate. That is no doubt why

Protestant and Catholic leaders in the past were ready to ban blasphemous speech; it was in error, and there is no social value in error. Every group in a society has its truths and is tempted even today to chill "blasphemous" speech that questions them.

But the free speech principle embodies the pragmatic theory of truth, which views it as the consensus result of a debate having no finite conclusion. Justice Oliver Wendell Holmes's famous "marketplace of ideas" reflects this principle. Even in science, today's truths may be replaced by a new version of reality as a result of future experimentation and discussion. Indeed, pragmatists see strong similarities between the realm of science and those of politics and literature.[13] They do not deny the reality of the earth, the planets, or the value of a flu shot, but they emphasize the equally compelling reality of socially constructed facts, such as the existence of money, the Federal Reserve System, and the truths of the Christian and Muslim religions.

Decades ago, the distinguished philosopher John Dewey also argued the case for pragmatism in science as well as politics. He said, "But in the practice of science, knowledge is an affair of *making* sure, not of grasping antecedently given sureties. What is already known, what is accepted as truth, is of immense importance. . . . But it is held subject to use, and is at the mercy of the discoveries which it makes possible."[14]

Dewey rejects the notion that discovery is the taking of something existing and fully formed.[15] He explains that when the Norsemen found America, there was no "discovery" in any creative sense unless and until the new land was employed to alter existing concepts.[16] He points out that the new map is part of reality just as is the newly discovered continent, and that the new map and the interpretations thereof are part of new knowledge.[17] Truth is not something found but something made and changed by the continuous process of discussion and inquiry.

Dewey elsewhere uses another simple but powerful example, taking the case of a man lost in the woods.[18] How to find his way home? Some would argue that the plan or idea of a route home is true if it matches up with reality, a reality out there somewhere. Dewey does not deny the existence of a physical reality; that would be silly. But how can the lost man test the truthfulness of his plan to get home? He cannot stand still and compare his plan or idea with reality.[19] Only when the plan has been used as a guide to action that has met with success is the plan deemed correct or true.[20] The plan is right because "it has, *through action*, worked out the state of things which it contemplated or intended."[21] Dewey concludes, "From this point of view verification and truth are two names for the same thing. We call it 'verification' when we regard it as process," the process of action, conversation, and testing.[22]

Charles Sanders Peirce, perhaps America's greatest philosopher, spoke of truth as that which a group of scientific experts or peers agrees to, i.e., reaches consensus upon, after investigation. John Dewey democratized that concept.[23] He rejected the notion that political opinion should rely principally on expert opinion rather than the give and take of common discourse.[24]

Christopher Lasch, in his last book, summarized the learning of Dewey (and his great colleague William James) on the value of free speech as follows: "It is only by subjecting our preferences and projects to the test of debate that we come to understand what we know and what we still need to learn. . . . The attempt to bring others around to our own point of view carries the risk, of course, that we may adopt their point of view instead. . . . Argument is risky and unpredictable, therefore educational."[25]

The greatest American jurist Justice Holmes agreed with the pragmatist position. In his famous dissent in *Abrams v. United States*, a free speech case, he supported the merits of free speech and asserted that "at any rate is the theory of our Constitution. It is an experiment, as all life is an experiment."[26]

The discussion to this point obviously does not mean that pragmatism takes the view that every belief is as good as every other. However, it does take the position that there are no transcendental foundations to our beliefs, no Platonic forms or essences that underlie the definition of truth.[27] Pragmatists discuss various alternatives in terms of specific advantages and disadvantages; they do not find answers in terms of an objective moral imperative. The solutions and answers are the result of a continuing "conversation," or process.[28]

The anti-pragmatist believes that we engage in human discourse in order to reach an end and to terminate the dialogue.[29] That approach takes a cynical view of the pragmatist.[30] The anti-pragmatist, who argues that ultimate agreement is the goal of conversation, "is like the basketball player who thinks that the reason for playing the game is to make baskets";[31] that interpretation mistakes the importance of baskets for the "end" of the process.[32] The anti-pragmatist accuses the pragmatist of lacking proof of his or her opinions and of being bound by appeal to the changing consensus of the community in which he or she resides. But in this age when religious faith is waning, and when faith in the objective reason of the age of enlightenment has also failed, we must continue with our conversations.

This does not mean that in relatively simple matters the conversation cannot reach a stopping point or agreement on terms.[33] In anything relatively complex or significant, however, the inquiry cannot be stopped without resort to coercion or terror. Changing conditions, changing parties, and new contingencies result in ever-newer interpretations. One hundred years ago, for example, Columbus was a hero; today it is difficult to mount a major event in his honor. Significant conversations are marked by this sort of interpretation and reinterpretation.

Philosopher Jacques Derrida captured this spirit in his arguments for deconstruction of text and for the relative unimportance of the writer's so-called "intent." Derrida's work reflects the influence of Jewish mysticism in this respect.[34] For example, some sages have argued that Moses transmitted only two commandments from God to the people of Israel. Rabbi Mendel of Rymanow replies that not even the first two commandments were revealed directly: "All that Israel heard was the *aleph* with which in the Hebrew text the first commandment begins."[35] The scholar Gershom Scholem explains that the consonant *aleph* represents merely the position of the throat when the sound is uttered.[36] To hear the *aleph is to hear no meaning*.[37] The people of Israel heard nothing more than *aleph* from God; everything thereafter was human interpretation and reinterpretation. There was no understandable, transcendental foundation to the religion revealed to the people of Israel.

John Dewey put it differently but emphasized the same point. He stated that certain truths (that is, tested ideas) "afford an effective method of dealing with questions arising apparently from unallied sources."[38] They become of great use and are the "eternal" truths of "current discussion."[39] But we cannot exaggerate the permanence of even such "truths." "When applied to new cases . . . the oldest of truths are to some extent remade."[40] He stated further, "Above all, it is in the region of moral truth that this perception stands out. Moral truths that are not recreated in application to the urgencies of the passing hour . . . are pernicious and misleading, *i.e.*, false."[41]

Free speech principles depend upon a pragmatic belief in the nature of truth. As Richard Posner puts it, "Truth is what free inquiry—unforced, undistorted, and uninterrupted—would eventually discover about the objects of inquiry. Since the process of inquiry never ends, this implies that truth always lies beyond our horizon: it is there but we aren't."[42] The test of time is important; in a sense, truth is that consensus which develops over time. But even a widely held consensus may not hold indefinitely. New ideas and new developments can break it, as Albert Einstein's discovery of relativity theory replaced the old Newtonian consensus. Ideas should be subjected to a Darwinian survival test mediated by vigorous free speech and inquiry that both moves toward a consensus or a changed consensus and makes the consensus reached more acceptable.[43]

The pragmatic approach is skeptical, but not completely so. That we now believe the earth is round but a thousand years ago believed it was flat does not mean the earth was then flat. Yet pragmatism, because of its reference to the role of consensus in defining truth, does tend to blur the distinction between fact and opinion.[44] As Posner stated, "truth" is a "process of belief formations that unfolds over time."[45]

This skepticism does not mean cynicism about the role of ideas and the clash of debate. The skepticism and pragmatism underlying the argument for free speech also involve, somewhat ironically, a deep faith in the worth and value of discussion, disagreement, and criticism. It is not a skepticism that entails any kind of nihilism about the impact of ideas. Although truth is always out there somewhere, beyond our ken, and absolutism is suspect, there is still an eighteenth-century enlightenment belief in the wonder and majesty of argument, disputation, and the quest for truth. This non-nihilistic skepticism is eloquently supported by Hilary Putnam in a recent book: "We see relativism not as a cure or a relief from the malady of 'lacking a metaphysical foundation', but rather see relativism *and* the desire for a metaphysical foundation as manifestations of the same disease. The thing to say to the relativist is that some things are true and some things are warranted and some things are reasonable, but of course we can only *say* so if we have an appropriate language. And we do have the language, and we can and do say so, even though that language does not itself rest on any metaphysical guarantee like Reason."[46]

He continues with a reference to Ludwig Wittgenstein:
"508: What can I rely on?
509: I really want to say that a language game is only possible if one trusts something. (I did not say 'can trust something')."[47]

Our dialogue rests not on some ineffable Reason; neither is it consumed by nihilism. We put our trust in others without certain guarantees.[48] Our trust is not naive; frequently we must check, verify, and probe. This uncertain process is difficult for most of us. Putnam asserts that frequently we struggle to seek either a transcendental guarantee or a totally subjectivist escape, but that neither is healthy.[49]

John Dewey argues that there are good and bad solutions to human problems; we find them through experiment and debate. He believes, as Peirce held in his two famous articles that began the pragmatist movement, that the solutions from authority, tenacity and transcendental Reason, do not work. We solve problems in ethics and science through hypothesis, experiment, trial, and debate. As a solution emerges, however, that solution itself will become unworkable as new facts and conditions emerge.[50]

Richard Posner puts the same thought in this manner:

> Pragmatist skepticism about "truth" might, for example, be thought to undermine the nation's commitment to free speech. If there is no truth "out there," how can free speech be defended by reference to its efficacy in bringing us nearer to truth? Actually this is not such a difficult question. If there is no truth out there, this

should make us particularly wary of people who claim to
have found the truth and who argue that further inquiry
would be futile. . . . There is *knowledge* if not ultimate
truth, and a fallibilist theory of knowledge emphasizes,
as preconditions to the growth of . . . knowledge, the
continual testing and retesting of accepted "truths."[51]

The pragmatic approach, in Dewey's opinion, necessarily
requires cooperative dialogue. This entails the democratization of ethical and political life. Knowledge and inquiry do
not grow from authority or the *diktat* of even a benevolent
tyrant. Pragmatists cannot prove the existence of objective
ethical norms, but norms can arise out of the process of dialogue. That dialogue does not start from a position of doubt-
ing everything;[52] the participants in the dialogue frequently
share a great number of factual and value beliefs. Out of the
debate and confrontation there frequently comes a new for-
mulation that satisfies the disputants. That "solution" may
involve the development of criteria not accepted or realized
at the outset of the discussion. But this scenario does not
mean that all disputes will be settled.[53]

The pragmatic view is not limited to purely rational, logical
debate. It recognizes that the search for elusive truth utilizes
rhetoric, metaphor, and imagery. The human mentality influences and is influenced by poetry, emotion, symbols, action,
and passion. Hence, the pragmatic view implies that protected
speech includes more than the syllogisms, abstract reason, and
the kinds of language found in academic journals.[54]

William James emphasized the passionate nature of
thought. Outside of science—and even *in* science—men and
women are confronted with the need to make decisions before the facts are in, and indeed frequently in situations where
brute facts do not exist and ambiguity prevails. In the moral,

religious, and political realms we continually make existential decisions in the absence of "facts" that can compel an answer. In science, creative geniuses advance theories and adhere to them in advance of the experimental data.[55] As James puts it, "Objective evidence and certitude are doubtless very fine ideals to play with, but where on this moonlit and dream-visited planet are they found?"[56] But James is not a nihilist: "But please observe, now, that when as empiricists we give up the doctrine of objective certitude, we do not give up the quest or hope for truth itself. We still pin our faith on its existence, and still believe that we gain an even better position towards it by systematically continuing to roll up experiences and think."[57]

James ends *The Will to Believe* with an existentialist passage from Fitzjames Stephen. This beautiful statement underlines the open-ended and emotive nature of the human conversation.

What do you think of yourself? What do you think of the world? . . . These are questions with which all must deal as it seems good to them. They are riddles of the Sphinx, and in some way or other we must deal with them. . . . In all important transactions of life we have to take a leap in the dark. . . . If we decide to leave the riddles unanswered, that is a choice; if we waiver in our answer that, too, is a choice: but whatever choice we make, we make it at our peril. If a man chooses to turn his back altogether on God and the future, no one can prevent him; no one can show beyond reasonable doubt that he is mistaken. If a man thinks otherwise and acts as he thinks, I do not see that any one can prove that *he* is mistaken. Each must act as he thinks best; and if he is wrong, so much the worst for him. We stand on a mountain pass in the midst of whirling snow and blinding mist, through which we get glimpses now and then of paths which may be deceptive. If we stand still we

shall be frozen to death. If we take the wrong road we
shall be dashed to pieces. We do not certainly know
whether there is any right one. What must we do? "Be
strong and of good courage." Act for the best. Hope
for the best, and take what comes. . . . If death ends all,
we cannot meet death better.[58]

CRITICS OF TRADITIONAL FREE SPEECH LIBERALISM

Modern radical critics of traditional free speech liberalism
likely will respond in the following manner: Although truth
is notoriously difficult to define or find, we all agree on some
things. The earth is round. The earth revolves around the sun.
Genocide is evil. Not even the most ardent civil libertarian is
an absolute skeptic about the search for truth. She or he will
agree that hateful speech about blacks, women, Jews, and
Hispanics is despicable. Those old friends of the First Amendment will no doubt fear that hateful speech may destroy the
sense of community that binds our society together. They will
concur that the assumptions of fact underlying hateful epithets—Jews plan to control the world, blacks are inferior,
women are subordinate to men—are false. I expect that civil
libertarians will not concede the remotest possibility that they
are in error here.

Therefore, since the truth is clear in this regard and false
words may do great damage, why protect false hateful speech?
We do not permit a school curriculum devoted to the flat-
earth science of a thousand years ago; it follows that racist
and sexist speech should be lawfully prohibited, despite the
First Amendment.

It is at this point that civil libertarians introduce "slippery
slope" arguments.[59] The arguments are of a familiar type. The

danger is that a policy that permits censorship based on content cannot be limited to the particular category chilled. The temptation of the courts and the executive branch will be to broaden the breach in the doctrine of content-neutrality. Censorship of racist speech may some day lead to the chilling of socialists, libertarians, Marxists, or critical legal studies scholars.

The response is usually that the courts and legislatures can easily distinguish between the unique category of sexist or racist speech and all other kinds of speech. Distinguished commentators have also argued that sexist and racist speech is uniquely condemnable. They make a communitarian argument: the purpose of the government is to preserve a coherent and acceptable set of values designed to bind citizens together in a condition of dignity and civil respect. This purpose is not some kind of external, superficial operation of government; rather, government should reinforce the deep-seated commonalities based on human worth that are natural to the American society. Racist speech, unlike all other categories of speech, is foreign and alien to the inherent purposes of the American society. Hence, loathsome speech should not be protected by the First Amendment.

The new theorists are, I believe, engaged in an intellectual pursuit that entails more than a slippery-slope risk. I define "slippery slope" as the danger that courts will take one breach in content-neutrality and, in the interests of uniformity and coherence, develop other breaches. As an example of slippery-slope reasoning, a court may argue that just as racist speech is emotionally inflammatory and is based on false premises about human nature and should therefore be lawfully censored, so too should the government censor comic books that are emotionally inflammatory and promote violence in the reader.

This slippery slope is a serious risk. It is one that should cause us concern with the new theorists' positions. But there is something even more ominous in their thinking, albeit related to the slippery-slope argument. They have accepted as a fundamental proposition that there are certain orthodoxies that a society and a government must accept and enforce in order to maintain worth and dignity. It is a proposition that was fundamental to Western society before the success of First Amendment principles. Indeed, it is the order of mind that free speech advocacy was designed to overthrow. One hundred years ago and earlier, it was commonplace to assume that society must preserve certain beliefs in order to maintain the worthy community.[60] For example, atheism was to be chilled (in earlier centuries by execution) since belief in God was a basis for the good society. Atheism was regarded as fundamentally alien to the societal consensus, a movement that would rend the fabric of society. There are many people today in our society who, while they may not recommend execution of atheists, nevertheless regard atheism as irrefutably evil and metaphysically contrary to the good society. The First Amendment restrains their ardor for censorship. The free speech principle inculcates in them a belief that even expressions of ultimate falsehood and depravity must not be censored.

As this example suggests, there is nothing to contain the philosophy that x category of speech, and only x, is false and dangerous and hence must be censored. No so-called neutral, truth-seeking principle will, without government compulsion, convince every faction, group, and party not to advance their deeply held convictions that y and z categories are also loathsome and must be suppressed, once political factions succeed in imposing their views on x.

The new theorists have adopted in modern dress the old societal theories that the free speech movements of the past centuries were designed to defeat. As Leonard Levy wrote, "Neither freedom of speech nor freedom of press could become a civil liberty until people believed that the truth of their opinions, especially their religious opinions, was relative rather than absolute."[61] It is clear, then, why the new theorists reject the Holmesian skepticism of the traditional civil libertarians. The move toward acceptance of new absolutes signals the eventual end of First Amendment liberalism. There can be no limit of absolutes to the category of racist or sexist speech. Once we admit a breach of content or viewpoint neutrality because racist speech is false and dangerous, we have to fight that battle on every other front as well. In every dispute we can expect the argument that the speech under threat of censorship is false, will lead to harm, and hence should be banned.

Indeed, it was just this kind of argument that was used in the fifties to attempt to ban communist speech.[62] The supporters of censorship asserted that communism was a deeply flawed doctrine that would lead to totalitarian evil. Now, even old apologists for communism admit that the censors were on target in their assessment of the falsity and danger of communist doctrine. Civil libertarians of the day argued that suppression would lead by various slippery-slope passages to censorship of good or noble ideas. Years earlier Holmes had argued that "only the emergency that makes it immediately dangerous to leave the correction of evil counsels to time warrants making any exception to the sweeping command [of the First Amendment]."[63]

If we ban racist speech, how then do we not move inexorably to the suppression of other unpopular thought, such as communist speech? The potential evil of communist propaganda is enormous. We have witnessed seventy years of failure, mass killings and attempted genocide by communist regimes, and the collapse of the communist regimes in the Soviet Union and Eastern Europe. Surely, the perversity and evil of totalitarian communist thought is as apparent to all of us as the evil of racist speech. There is no principled method of separating the two for First Amendment purposes, once we accept the premise that demonstrated falsity is the test for diminished First Amendment protection.

The new critics of the First Amendment condemn the skepticism of traditional liberalism. They are on target in this attack, because they have correctly identified the heart of First Amendment theory. They strike a receptive chord among many, because today in America, as was true when John Stuart Mill lived, we live in an age "destitute of faith, but terrified at skepticism."[64]

Absolutism in any form is fundamentally contrary to First Amendment doctrine. If certain truths are correct beyond peradventure, then what is the point of free debate, and the marketplace of ideas, in a marketplace where truth and value has been correctly determined? Mill identified the position of the new critics when he observed over one hundred years ago: "Strange that they should imagine that they are not assuming infallibility when they acknowledge that there should be free discussion on all subjects which can possibly be *doubtful* but think that some particular principle or doctrine should be forbidden to be questioned because it is *so certain*, that is, because *they are certain* that it is certain."[65]

The new critics are generally men and women on the left wing of the political spectrum. But their assault on First Amendment skepticism is shared by conservatives; Willmore Kendall is a good example. He has argued that a strong version of the First Amendment assumes that "society is . . . a *debating* club."[66] Kendall disagreed, asserting that "[s]ocieties . . . cherish a whole series of goods—among others . . . the *living* of the truth they believe themselves to embody already."[67] He also claimed that a First Amendment–driven society will "descend . . . into progressive breakdown of those common premises upon which alone a society can conduct its affairs by discussion."[68]

A far greater figure than either Kendall or the new critics argued long ago for the need to exercise censorship in order to achieve a good and just society. Plato, in *The Republic*, had no difficulty reaching a firm belief in what was objectively good, just, and true.[69] He emphasized the values of censorship in the areas of nurture and education in order to assure such goals. As he put it, "Then the first thing will be to establish a censorship of the writers of fiction, and . . . reject the bad."[70] One of the standards will be the elimination of any tales that create a fear of death, because inculcation of the virtues of bravery in battle is important for the guardians of the just society.[71] Further, literature that praises laughter must be eliminated, because the guardians must be sober and solemn.[72] Third, lying will be prohibited—except by the rulers, who are to have that privilege.[73] Also, literature will be monitored to assure that the youth will be temperate, obedient to commanders, and controlled in "sensual pleasures."[74] In addition, no tale that ascribes evil or vicious acts to the gods will be permitted.[75]

In a famous passage, Plato recommends the expulsion of playwrights from the ideal state, since, as he curiously puts it, actors frequently play the role of evil or weak men and women, and this is somehow a debasing practice.[76] Next he addresses music, demanding that all but stirring and martial airs be expunged from the permitted kinds of melody.[77] All of this (and more) will create a just, virtuous, and courageous citizenry and ruling class, whose members will be in harmony with justice. One of the felicitous results, Plato observed, will be an indisposition to frequent the law courts or to become lawyers.[78]

Even where absolutes are accepted, there is a First Amendment fallback position. Mill argued that the truth cannot be understood unless debated;[79] the Jewish Talmud is an example (far older than Mill) of this position. The great scholar Rabbi Adin Steinsaltz has noted that the Talmud is "the only sacred book in all of world culture that permits and even encourages the student to question it."[80] As Edward Alexander has said, "The talmudic practice of preserving . . . rejected arguments . . . might in fact be the only stable foundation for a just reliance on the *victorious* doctrine."[81]

But in the hurly burly world of politics and power, the fallback position is weak once the society accepts the view that for First Amendment purposes certain thoughts and ideas are politically correct or incorrect. The burden, then, is on proponents of incorrect views to prove that they should be able to continue to speak falsely. At best, they will avail themselves of a view along the lines of First Amendment commercial speech doctrine. That body of jurisprudence holds that although commercial speech gets some First Amendment protection, it is diluted. Since commercial speech is considered easily verifiable by the government, the court permits the government to ban false speech or to monitor and correct misleading commercial speech.

I have emphasized the skeptical underpinnings of First Amendment theory in the context of a free market for ideas and opinions.[82] That is, we are fundamentally skeptical about the ability of courts to distinguish areas where truth is recognized from those where there is fundamental inability to reach truth in some convincing sense. There are other reasons, apart from the rationale of debate as the surety of an open and free market in ideas, commonly advanced for the First Amendment. One purpose or goal is advancement of human autonomy or self-realization, whether of speaker or listener.[83] Free speech, liberally interpreted, permits the flowering of the human personality. Certainly, this is one of the commonly advanced purposes of a strong interpretation of the First Amendment, but it has its limits as an argument.

I doubt that many would argue that racist and sexist speech advances human autonomy or worthy self-expression. I take it as given and true that such speech is degrading and false, that it advances the most bestial elements of the human personality. Here again, the argument that can create a First Amendment wall around such loathsome speech is skepticism of the kind discussed above. That is, once we concede that certain kinds of self-expression and forms of human autonomy are based on false and grotesque assumptions and hence should be censored, there is no principle that can contain the search for both self-expression that is worthy and self-expression that is not. For example, the Roman Catholic Church views homosexuality as loathsome and sinful. Many in the church do not view the issue as debatable and subject to reasonable difference; it is a matter of "God's law." Do we then ban speech advocating that lifestyle?

Once we admit that there are true orthodoxies on which courts can reach closure, such as that racist speech is false and harmful and hence must be banned, the courts will consider all other issues on which certain groups consider speech to be abominable. Executives will nominate judges, and legislatures will confirm them, based on the nominees' notions of what is acceptable speech and what is not. Inevitably, the courts will begin to censor human self-expression and self-realization that is within a sphere of doubt and debate as to its truthfulness and worthiness, even though advocates deny that the sphere of doubt exists.

Another reason for a strong version of the First Amendment is the contention that free speech is essential to the democratic process.[84] This expresses the fairly obvious concept that men and women, political parties, and interest groups must communicate and debate in order for the democratic process to proceed and flourish. But the cogent proposition may always be made that certain ideas and philosophies are repugnant to a worthy democratic polity. Racism, sexism, and the domination of minorities and women by white males are conditions that, if successful, will create or maintain a society that is hateful and racist rather than democratic and free. But here again, we censor such speech at our peril, because of the fallibility of the human intellect. There is, to repeat the argument made above, no principled method—once we accept the philosophy that the courts may censor speech they regard as harmful to the democratic process—to contain the inevitable future attempts to censor all ideas and opinions that the courts fear will destroy the democratic process as they see it at a given moment. To give one example: Many in America believe that right-wing religious fundamentalism is loathsome. Does it follow that we should chill their speech?

As indicated above, free speech has been justified as, first, a method to facilitate truth-seeking (but not, as some naively assume, to assure it); second, a means for assuming human autonomy and dignity; and third, a facilitator of the democratic process. On analysis, human fallibility and the elusive nature of truth underlie all three principles and their corollaries. Because we cannot be certain as to what opinions help or harm democracy, we should not censor that which we consider offensive to the democratic ideal. Because we cannot be certain as to what concepts advance or demean human autonomy, we should permit vigorous debate. Needless to say, the same skepticism supports a free market in order to forward the pursuit of truth—contingently, out there, somewhere.

In summary, the new critics allege that once society reaches a consensus, as in the area of racist or sexist speech, it is the duty of government to sustain true belief and wipe out false opinion. This is a principle that is impossible to contain. In the first place, it is impossible to achieve infallibility in the judgment that a consensus has been reached. Since dissent itself is at issue, there will always be those dissenters who insist that truth has not been ascertained. Second, even if only one individual in all mankind disagrees on an issue, to use the famous Mill example, the truth cannot be said to have been infallibly ascertained.[85] Third and most important, once we grant that society can infallibly pick certain opinions as "noxious,"[86] censorship will quickly extend to all areas that majorities, or powerful minority interest groups, consider dangerous. The free speech principle must permit grotesque and nasty speech, because society in the domain of speech cannot be half skeptical and half infallible. We cannot infallibly choose the subjects that are legitimately debatable and those that are not. Once the boundary between the acceptable and the unacceptable is open for judicial scrutiny and legislative action, self-interested groups will forever battle to legitimate censorship in one area after another.

The strong First Amendment position I advocate is admittedly a difficult one for society to maintain. My best comparison is to the unicyclist on the high wire: it is a difficult balancing act. We maintain a strong version of the First Amendment not because the truth or usefulness of an idea or mode of self-expression cannot in many areas be ascertained to some degree of certainty. That is, we are not total skeptics. Rather, we maintain it because we lack the capacity to distinguish areas of certainty, more or less, from those where what now seems truth will in the future seem elusive and changeable. Perhaps more importantly, we are fearful of the dangers of handing to courts the ability to decide what areas possess or can reach knowledge having some measure of certitude. That skepticism extends to areas of science, art, economics, and politics. It also extends to the role of speech in facilitating the self-realization of speaker or listener. And it extends to the role of speech in facilitating the political process. Once we accept that debate and inquiry must end in certain areas, we cannot limit that principle. Litigators and the courts will forever seek out subjects upon which debate should end. The search will be ceaseless, and the areas of censorship will forever expand.

PRAGMATISM AND FIRST AMENDMENT DOCTRINE

The process of discussion and debate is, as I have argued, essential to the preservation of the open, liberal society.[87] It is at the heart of the definition of truth. It is a central institution of freedom.[88]

The Supreme Court's belief in the pragmatic praxis explains much of technical First Amendment doctrine. In particular, it explains the Court's resolute protection of political speech, the very core and center of free speech doctrine. No matter how resolutely stupid the political opinion, no matter how hatefully a candidate expresses himself or herself, the court will protect the speech from censorship.

In the recent Supreme Court decision *R.A.V. v. City of St. Paul*,[89] the majority opinion appeared to move toward the theory that speech is valuable in itself.[90] The Court threw out a city crime ordinance that prohibited the display of symbols of hate speech, concluding by a bare majority that even fighting words, a previously non-protected variety of speech, were in fact protected to some extent by First Amendment principles. As Justice Antonin Scalia stated, "sometimes [fighting words] are quite expressive indeed."[91] The legislature could ban all fighting words, but it could not selectively ban such words as racial epithets while permitting insults directed at union membership or political affiliation. Such viewpoint-selectivity was impermissible.[92] The four concurring justices argued that the city was justified in selecting hate speech as a particularly dangerous category of fighting words, requiring special treatment.[93]

We see a turn away from the pragmatic philosophy at work in many areas where full First Amendment protection does not apply. By that I mean that the Court weakens First Amendment protection in subjects where it believes that it has found "hard" truth and in which there is, therefore, no need for further debate. For example, commercial speech receives less First Amendment protection than political speech.[94] One of the frequent explanations given for this distinction, although admittedly not the only one, is that the truth of advertising is easier to ascertain than in the realm of politics. Truth in this context is a hard, objective, "scientific," governmentally determinable, "out there" truth: for example, *x* toothpaste does not clean. Obscenity is not protected because the Court has determined that obscene speech is not true or valid; it is rather, a debased coin not worthy of protection by the First Amendment. If the speech can be shown to have some "serious" purpose, that is, one "worthy" of continued debate, then it is protected.[95] Truth or falsity here is a moral truth or falsity, and the Court has determined that "obscene" literature is morally false.

The pragmatist would consider the truth component of both discourses, commercial or moral, to be the subjects of the same kind of process—or rather, to be defined by the same sort of process—to wit discussion, debate, and temporary consensus. The Court has decided in both cases, commercial speech and obscene speech, that the debate should end, because a "final," correct, judicial judgment can and should be reached. (There is a difference, that commercial speech gets limited protection, obscene speech none. But the difference is illusory: false commercial speech is not protected, whereas serious speech that is otherwise obscene *is* protected, because it has an aesthetic truth value.)

Core political speech is protected from judicial *diktat* because of an enthusiastic endorsement of the pragmatic notion that political truth is ideally a process of continuous debate

rather than a closed-loop, judicially discernable modality ending in the Truth. It is a pragmatic philosophical approach that
leads the Court and commentators to desire protection of the
core political areas; it is an abandonment of that approach in
other areas that leads to lessened protection there.

Defamation is an area where the courts have decided that
reputation is so great a value that truth is better "established"
by litigation than debate. That is, in order to protect reputation, the courts will determine the truth or falsity of the
alleged defamatory remark. Pragmatic faith in the workings
of the market for ideas is suspended because of the courts'
concern for the reputation of the plaintiff. (Even so, the Supreme Court raises high hurdles against success in suits where
the plaintiff is a public figure, so as to preserve the vigor of
public criticism of public figures.)

There is a consensus in modern liberal society that democracy is a positive value and that dictatorship, or Nazism, is
evil. We have had overwhelmingly sufficient experience in recent decades to believe the conclusions to be sound. Yet the
Court permits, under First Amendment principles, advocacy
of Nazism but not false toothpaste ads or false claims of proxy
contestants. In some fashion, the Court believes truth is hard,
objective, out there to be found, and indeed to be found in
the commercial advertisement area but not in the political.
Yet some political "truths" are as solid as scientific truths. All
of us "know" that Nazism is a false idea, albeit debated by
some skinheads, in a sense more certain than that in which
data about a toothpaste ad or even a principle of physics can
be disputed. The First Amendment interpretation is "fiercely"
pragmatic, so to speak, in the core political area but not in
certain other areas, such as commercial speech and obscenity.
Another explanation, at least in the example of Nazis mentioned above, may be that no one takes the viability of Nazism
in the United States seriously. However, as intellectual and

political leaders take the threat of racism more seriously, the effort to ban racist speech grows.

Rorty states, "Imagine . . . that a few years from now you open your copy of the *New York Times* and read that philosophers, in convention assembled, have unanimously agreed that values are objective, science rational, truth a matter of correspondence to reality, and so on. Recent breakthroughs in semantics and metaethics, the report goes on, have caused the last remaining noncognitivists in ethics to recant."[96] No doubt the public response would be amused, to say the least. The Court, in a sense, has done this in the area of obscenity and other low-value areas of speech. That is, it has approved a consensus that certain art is true and beautiful, but that certain art is not and hence should be censored. Indeed, some of the tensions in First Amendment law through the decades have turned on the community of judges, lawyers, and others agreeing, or almost agreeing, on Truths. In the 1950s and earlier decades, many in society agreed that communism was a false doctrine; hence, efforts were made to limit First Amendment doctrine for that speech.[97] But many intellectuals did not believe that communism was false, or at least they were willing to take the free speech risk in that area.[98] Today there is perhaps a wider consensus among all groups that racist or sexist speech is objectively false. Minority and feminist spokespersons are not necessarily willing to concede the pragmatic notions of truth and discussion when it comes to propositions about race and gender. They are convinced that they can draw the line in this area without jeopardizing free speech in other domains. They do not believe that it is relativistic interpretation all the way down[99]—hence the push to narrow First Amendment doctrine in the area.

This last point bears repetition and some amplification. Truth in the pragmatic sense rests upon consensus, although not a converging consensus based upon a certain harmony in life and nature. In the scientific world, that consensus is based upon agreed-upon modes of discussion and agreement in the scientific community. A similar process, albeit with more strife and less agreement on the ground rules of consensus, occurs in the larger political community. That consensus is never final and is always subject to further debate and reformulation. Yet in certain areas, the political or legal community does believe that it has reached a final agreement. Hence, as mentioned above, we see the Court's determination that obscenity is regulatable. In the 1950s many argued for a similar decision in the area of communist speech. But intellectuals and other cultural leaders never reached an overwhelming consensus about the allegedly irredeemable vices of communism. Our society may be reaching just such a consensus in the areas of racist and pornographic speech. If so, the Supreme Court may ultimately be persuaded. Rorty's convention of philosophers, in different form, will have met, and the public response will not be ironic. A dangerous principle will be established (or perhaps, more accurately, expanded from its base in obscenity and defamation law) that when society reaches a consensus, it is permissible to cut that realm off from the protection of free speech.

PRAGMATISM AND RELIGION

In this chapter we have argued for the skeptical foundations of a liberal, even libertarian, support of free speech. But there is an important religious objection to a secular, non-foundationalist basis for toleration and diversity. Ian S. Markham, in an important book, *Plurality & Christian Ethics*, has put it as follows: "Once God goes . . . [t]olerance becomes an end in itself. On this account, all society consists of is a group of individuals who must coexist in a moral vacuum with minimum interaction."[100] Markham then argues that since for the secularist truth is relative and not anchored in founda-tions, "[p]ublic discourse becomes an exercise in assertion, not discussion."[101] Hence, reason is destroyed, and power be-comes the measure. However, the religious person, Christian, Jew, or Muslim, believes in a fundamental truth. For them, therefore, discussion is vital and meaningful, not merely an exercise in nihilistic assertion-mongering.[102]

The discussion of pragmatism in this chapter demonstrates the weakness in the contention that the secularist cannot rea-sonably argue, reason, experiment, or pay sensitive attention to data. Indeed, it would tread old ground to refer to the religious wars of yesterday as a vehicle for raising questions about the relative roles of arbitrary assertion in religious vs. secular discourse. As Stephen Holmes writes, "Liberals did not invent domination, exploitation intimidation, arm-twisting or terror. Likewise they did not invent war. . . . Fi-nally, slavery can plausibly be considered the most instrumental of all human relations. But predatory groups re-duced their weak and conquered neighbors long before lib-eralism was on the scene."[103]

But Markham's criticism of the secular, although eloquent, is not the real point of his excellent, slender book. The im-portant points are the arguments he makes for the role mod-ern religion (and more particularly in his case, Christianity) can play in legitimating a pragmatic basis for free speech. He argues that the Christian belief in a transcendental final goal and aim in life is not only consistent with, but supportive of, a pragmatic approach to free speech. This contention, obvi-ously, was not the mainstream position of the Catholic hier-archy in the past. Nevertheless, he cogently argues that the modern church is pragmatic in a particular religious context.

His historical point is that religion in America has been fundamentally influenced by the experience of plurality (his word for pluralism):[104] "[T]he United States has made a cultural discovery. It has found good religious reasons why we ought to affirm plurality. . . . The nation of immigrants was forced, right from the start, to engage with plurality. And slowly a culture emerged that was both religious and tolerant."

These are his three principal philosophical arguments:

1. "Humans are sinful. . . . Therefore we must be consistently humble and sensitive to the possibility of error."[105] He asserts dramatically that religion has "been affected by sin." This is a modern view, not shared by Christians of past centuries. This means that God's revelation has been rendered ambiguous by human sin.[106]

2. Related to the first point is the eschatological condition. We see as through a glass darkly. As Richard J. Neuhaus puts it, "nobody has the correct fit between the ultimacies of God's self-revelation in Christ and the penultimacies of the ordering of our political life."[107] God knows the best political solution, but until that is realized, the church must "contribute to the public dialogue in appropriate humility, ready and willing to learn from others."[108]

3. "When we become too certain, we imagine that we are God. This sin of hubris consists in the pretension that our partial insights are complete truths. . . . On this view dialogue is not an optional extra for theism, but a religious imperative."[109] In this regard Neuhaus points out, "Respect for the dignity of the other person created in the image of God requires that we do not silence or exclude him but try to persuade him."[110]

At the beginning of this chapter we pointed out that the modern secular age does not encompass a unified concept of belief. Hence there is debate and diversity. But Neuhaus has argued that a unified religious conception does not require "monism." He states that God has written pluralism and diversity into life. Therefore, even if everyone on earth became Christian, there would still be immense variousness. He also points out that belief in God does not necessitate uniform consensus on such lesser domains of truth as law, medicine, and "how to make a really good martini."[111]

Neuhaus also states that religious faith and reason are not incompatible. He cites St. Augustine to the effect that the religious, or certainly Christians, do not sacrifice reason to faith. Faith is not arbitrary, and reason and faith support each other. The crucial point he makes is that the religious can enter into a dialogue of reason with the secular. Both operate by common rules of logic; the religious as well as the secular agree that two plus two equals four.[112]

These are important arguments. They enlist religious believers in the pragmatic free speech dialogue. They come full circle, in a way, and link up with Wittgenstein's thesis, discussed above, that we converse not by way of nihilistic assertion but with reason (lower case), tolerance, and trust. But although there is trust, we cannot be foolish. The secular pragmatist knows that our language game (Wittgenstein jargon for our human dialogue) lacks transcendental justification but that it is what we have. The believer in God cannot free the human condition from error. For both, the "sin of hubris consists in the pretension that our partial insights are complete truths that need no connection or clarification from insights elsewhere."[113]

Ironically the sin of hubris is today committed by many of the radical critics of the old liberal interpretation of the First Amendment. They have exalted certain "truths" as so fundamental as to be beyond criticism. Examples are affirmative-action quotas, the right to abortion on demand, and the evils of pornography. As some intellectuals in the American Catholic Church and other religious groups move toward an acceptance of free speech philosophy in America, the new critics of a vigorous First Amendment are moving toward a nonreligiously based postmodern form of absolutism.

NOTES

1. Thomas L. Pangle, *The Ennobling of Democracy* 210 (1992) [hereinafter Pangle].
2. *Id.* at 210 (quoting Benedict Spinoza, *Theological-Political Treatise* ch. 20).
3. Professor Holmes writes: "The notion that skepticism poses a massive threat to society has remained a commonplace among antiliberals since Maistre's time." *Stephen Holmes, The Anatomy of Antiliberalism* 24 (1993).
4. Pangle, *supra* note 1, at 209.
5. *See generally* Jürgen Habermas, *The Philosophical Discourse of Modernity,* (Frederick G. Lawrence, trans., 1987).
6. *Id.*
7. Richard Rorty, *Contingency, Irony and Solidarity* 44 (1989) [hereinafter *Contingency*].
8. *Id.* at 3.
9. Rorty, of course, is not asserting that "atoms, wave packages, etc.," are creations of the human mind. Richard Rorty, *Philosophy and the Mirror of Nature* 345 (1979).
10. *Contingency, supra* note 7, at 46.
11. Isaiah Berlin, *Four Essays on Liberty* 172 (1969). Berlin describes the Enlightenment belief in the power of a universalist pure reason (as contrasted to the pragmatist's beliefs). He quotes Auguste Comte, "who asked 'If we do not allow free thinking in chemistry or biology, why should we allow it in morals or politics?' " *Id.* at 151. Berlin continues with his description of this kind of thinking: "Why indeed? If it makes sense to speak of political truths—assertions of social ends which all men, because they are men, must, once they are discovered, agree to be such; and if, as Comte believed, scientific method will in due course reveal them; then—what case is there for freedom of opinion or action—at least as an end in itself, and not merely as a stimulating intellectual cli-

mate, either for individuals or for groups?" *Id.* Berlin asks, "Can it be that Socrates and the creators of the central Western tradition [who believed that all men and women have one purpose and nature] in ethics and politics who followed him have been mistaken . . . ?" *Id.* at 154.

12. *Contingency, supra* note 7, at 51–2.

13. Richard Rorty, *Objectivity, Relativism, and Truth* 54 (1991) [hereinafter *Objectivity*].

14. John Dewey, *Experience and Nature* 154 (1926).

15. *Id.* at 156.

16. *Id.*

17. *Id.*

18. *The Philosophy of John Dewey* 194–98 (Joseph Ratner, ed., 1928) [hereinafter Ratner].

19. *Id.* at 196–7.

20. *Id.* at 197.

21. *Id.*

22. *Id.* at 199.

23. John P. Diggins, *The Promise of Pragmatism* 236 (1994).

24. Hilary Putnam, *Renewing Philosophy* 188–9 (1992) [hereinafter *Renewing*].

25. Christopher Lasch, *The Revolt of the Elites* 170–1 (1995).

26. 250 U. S. 616, 624 (1919).

27. Richard Rorty, *Consequences of Pragmatism* 164 (1982) [hereinafter *Consequences*].

28. *Id.* at 166–8.

29. *Id.* at 170.

30. *Id.* at 172.

31. *Id.*

32. Consequences, *supra* note 27, at 172.

33. *Id.* at xli.

34. *Habermas, supra* note 5, at 182–3.

35. *Id.* at 183 (quoting Gershom Scholem, *On the Kabbalah and Its Symbolism* 30 [1965]).

36. *Id.*

37. *Id.*

38. Ratner, *supra* note 18, at 240.

39. *Id.*

40. *Id.* at 241.

41. *Id.*

42. Richard Posner, *The Problems of Jurisprudence* 114 (1990) [hereinafter Posner].

43. *Id.*

44. *Id.*

45. *Id.*

46. *Renewing, supra* note 24, at 177.

47. *Id.* at 177 quoting Ludwig Wittgenstein, *On Certainty* (1969).

48. *Id.*

49. *Renewing, supra* note 24, at 177.

50. *Id.* at 186. The two articles, "How to Make Our Ideas Clear" and "The Fixation of Belief," appear in *Collected Papers of Charles Sanders Peirce, Vol. 5, Pragmatism and Pragmaticism,* ed. Charles Harsthorne and Paul Weiss (Cambridge, Mass.: Harvard University Press, 1965).

51. Posner, *supra* note 42, at 466 (emphasis added).

52. Hilary Putnam, *Words and Life* 175 (1994).

53. *Id.* at 176.

54. Richard Posner, *What Has Pragmatism to Offer Law?*, 63 S. Cal. L. Rev. 1653, 1662 (1990).

55. *See Renewing, supra* note 24, at 192–3.

56. William James, *The Will to Believe* 14, first published in 1897 (Longmans, Green and Co. 1927).

57. *Id* at 17.

58. *Id.* at 30–1. James is quoting from Fitzjames Stephen, *Liberty, Equality, Fraternity* (London: Smith, Elder, 1874).

59. John Nowak et al., *Constitutional Law* 836 (3d ed. 1986).

60. Leonard Levy, *Emergence of a Free Press* 5 (1985).

61. *Id.*

62. *See, e.g.,* Dennis v. United States, 341 U.S. 494 (1951); Yates v. United States, 353 U.S. 298 (1957).

63. Abrams v. United States, 250 U.S. 616, 630–1 (1919) (Holmes, J., dissenting).

64. John Stuart Mill, *On Liberty* ch. II (D. Spitz, ed., 1975) at 22 (quoting Thomas Carlyle, *Memoirs of the Life of Scott*).

65. *Id.*

66. *Id.* at 162.

67. *Id.*

68. *Id.* at 164–5.

69. Plato, *The Republic in* The Portable Plato 353 (Scott Buchanan, ed., 1977).

70. *Id.*

71. *Id.* at 364.

72. *Id.* at 368.

73. *Id.* at 369.

74. *Id.* at 370.

75. *Id.* at 373.

76. *Id.* at 383.

77. *Id.* at 384–6.

78. *Id.* at 402.

79. *Mill, supra* note 64, at 34–5.

80. Edward Alexander, *A Talmud for Americans,* 90 Commentary, July 1990, at 27, 30.

81. *Id.*

82. *See* Abrams v. United States, 250 U.S. 616, 630 (1919) (Holmes, J., dissenting).

83. *See e.g.* Martin H. Redish, *Freedom of Expression: A Critical Analysis* 11–29 (1984); Ralph K. Winter, *A First Amendment Over-View*, 55 Brooklyn L. Rev. 71 (1989).

84. Alexander Meiklejohn, *Free Speech and Its Relation to Self-Government* (1948); Robert Bork, *Neutral Principles and Some First Amendment Problems,* 47 Ind. L. J. 1 (1971).

85. Mill, *supra* note 64, at 18.

86. *Id.* at 23.

87. Rorty does point out that free discussion is the "sort which goes on when the press, the judiciary, the elections, and the universities are free, social mobility is frequent and rapid, literacy is universal, higher education is common, and peace and wealth have made possible the leisure necessary to listen to lots of different people and think about what they say." *Contingency, supra* note 7, at 84. If we push this observation to its fullest, there is no society on the face of the globe where free discussion is currently possible. I believe a better interpretation, a more "pragmatic" approach (herein a bit of mild deconstruction of text) would view these con-

ditions as an idealized version of the imperfect liberal political societies extant in the United States and parts of Europe. There is no doubt, however, that Rorty would want a radical egalitarianism in the *physical* conditions of society, such as equalization of wealth. *See* Richard Rorty, *Essays on Heidegger and Others* 190–1 (1991) [hereinafter *Essays*], where he calls for income equality but insists on the continued need for free speech.

88. *Essays, supra* note 87, at 190.

89. 112 S. Ct. 2538 (1992). In *Wisconsin v. Mitchell*, 508 U.S. 476 (1993) the Court held that penalty-enhancement statutes are constitutional under the First Amendment. These are statutes where the sentence for a crime such as battery, etc., is increased because the defendant selected the victim because of his or her race, religion, color, disability, sexual orientation, national origin, or ancestry. For a discussion of this case see Franklyn S. Haiman, *Speech Acts and the First Amendment*, ch. 5 (1993).

90. The doctrine was set forth by the Supreme Court in *Chaplinsky v. New Hampshire*, 315 U.S. 568, 572 (1942). The Court permitted the regulation of speech that could cause immediate breach of the peace. It also permitted regulation of speech that caused emotional harm. The latter doctrine is no longer good law. *See e.g.*, Cohen v. California, 403 U.S. 15 (1971). The former doctrine has been diluted and weakened by more recent cases. *See e.g.*, Terminiello v. Chicago 337 U.S. 1 (1949), Gooding v. Wilson, 405 U.S. 518 (1972).

91. *R.A.V. v. City of St. Paul*, 112 S. Ct. 2538, 2543–4 (1992).

92. *Id.* at 2547.

93. *Id.* at 2553 (White, J., concurring in judgment, and joined by Blackmun and O'Connor, JJ., and joined by Stevens, J., except as to Part I(A)); *Id.* at 2561 (Blackmun, J., concurring in judgment); *Id.* at 2561–2 (Stevens, J., concurring in judgment, and joined as to Part I by White and Blackmun, JJ.).

94. *See* Nicholas Wolfson, *Corporate First Amendment Rights and the SEC* 7–37 (1990).

95. Laurence H. Tribe, *American Constitutional Law* 904–20 (2d cd. 1988) [hereinafter Tribe].

96. Objectivity, *supra* note 13, at 43.

97. *See* Tribe, *supra* note 95, at 845–9.

98. *See* Paul Johnson, *Modern Times: The World from the Twenties to the Eighties* 252 (1983).

99. Richard Rorty, *Feminism and Pragmatism*, 30 Mich. Q. Rev. 231, 236, 244 (1991).

100. Ian S. Markham, *Plurality & Christian Ethics* 154 (1994) [hereinafter Markham].

101. *Id.* at 158.

102. Markham relies heavily on the writings of Richard John Neuhaus. *See*, e.g., R. Neuhaus, *The Naked Public Square* (1984).

103. Stephen Holmes, *The Anatomy of Liberalism* 245 (1994).

104. Markham, *supra* note 100, at 194.

105. *Id.* at 182.

106. *Id.*

107. *Id.* at 182 quoting from R.J. Neuhaus, *The Ambiguities of "Christian America,"* Concordia Journal 291–2 (July 1991).

108. *Id.* at 183.

109. *Id.* at 183–4.

110. Richard J. Neuhaus, *Why We Can Get Along*, 60 First Things 27 at 31 (Feb. 1996).

111. *Id.*

112. *Id.*

113. Markham, *supra* note 100, at 183. In a November 1996 issue of *First Things*, R. Neuhaus said some intemperate things about the American democratic system. His earlier words, quoted in the text, should, instead, be his guide.

CHAPTER 3

HATE SPEECH

A considerable body of persuasive legal literature supports the thesis that racist or sexist hate speech should receive reduced, or even no, protection under the First Amendment.[1] As we have seen in Chapter 2, the arguments are coherent and powerful. The empirical premises for the new First Amendment theory are, first, the scientific falsity of explicit or implicit racial or sexual stereotyping; and second, the harm such speech does to the victim. The person who is called "kike," "nigger," or "fag" suffers emotional humiliation and personal loss of dignity.[2] The victim feels threatened, humiliated, and diminished. It is asserted that he or she may suffer temporary or permanent psychological harm. Further, such expression, it is again argued, tears the weave of the community in which the speech is made, breaks down civil discourse, and incites weak-minded onlookers to similar thoughts and words. Finally, the ideational content of the utterance is minimal.

The traditional civil-libertarian response is predictable.[3] The First Amendment is designed to protect disgusting speech from the censorship of government. The offensiveness of the speech in question is never a reason for removing it from protection of the First Amendment. There are the usual exceptions—e.g., fighting words,[4] obscenity,[5] defamation,[6] speech too closely "brigaded" with forbidden conduct[7]—but otherwise the government must be viewpoint-neutral. At this point, critics of the traditional discourse ask the cogent question, Why should racist speech, which all enlightened men and women will admit is based upon false premises, be permitted? The factual assumptions underlying hate speech are to the effect that blacks, Jews, or women are inferior, stupid, greedy, or inherently violent. Both critics and traditionalists in the civil liberties community agree that the assumptions are false. The bigotry expressed in such racist remarks is based on "facts" on a par with the assumption that the world is flat. Moreover, traditionalists and critics, I submit, agree that the hatred expressed by such speech serves no socially redeeming value.

We have already considered in Chapter 2 arguments for continuing to protect hate speech under the First Amendment. In this chapter we consider additional arguments for protecting such speech from censorship.

The arguments are somewhat complex, and so we summarize them. To begin with, we point out that it is difficult if not impossible to limit censorship to the four-letter epithet. There is an expansive body of highbrow, fancy literature and philosophy that denigrates minorities, women, and gays; yet censorship of such works as *The Merchant of Venice* would be a draconian step few would endorse. However, if we limit censorship to the epithet, we create a two-tier approach: chilling of blue-collar muck and preservation of upper-crust mud. Second, much of what passes for debate in the intellectual and political community is redolent with emotion, insult, imagery, ridicule, and passion. (Remember the day when Patrick Buchanan presented a stuffed parrot to his audience to illustrate his contempt for then-Senator Bob Dole's alleged borrowing of his ideas?) The model of a free market of ideas limited to bloodless, cerebral cogitation is too limited to encompass the reality of discourse. Hence, to complain about racial and sexist speech because it is emotionally charged and low in ideational content is not very convincing.

Third, we address the contention that hate speech causes emotional, societal, and psychological harm and therefore should be censored. We argue that the purpose of free speech protection is to safeguard speech that the government views as harmful. Any other approach would permit the government to be the arbiter of what ideas are safe. Fourth, we consider the position that one-on-one hate speech—as it were, "in-your-face" hate speech—is in a different category from hate speech directed to the public, such as offensive books and television. We reject that distinction, short of the Brandenburg doctrine that permits regulation of speech that reasonably threatens imminent physical harm.

Fifth, we evaluate the relationship of defamation doctrine to hate speech. The two areas of disagreeable speech bear certain similarities to each other. We acknowledge that defamation-law doctrine—to wit, false statements of fact harmful to reputation are sometimes actionable—lends support to critics of a strong version of First Amendment protection of hate speech. Such critics can argue that hate speech is inherently false and, analogous to defamation doctrine, should be censored. We argue that defamation doctrine, although obviously an ancient and established jurisprudence, chills free speech. We further argue that the fact-versus-opinion distinction in defamation law—false facts are actionable, allegedly erroneous opinions are not—is a dangerous and frequently impossible distinction. Moreover, application of that approach to hateful speech outside of the traditional defamation area would permit a vast expansion of dangerous censorship. We would protect false "facts" as well as false opinions. Finally, we consider the role of education and hate speech. We argue that "politically correct" speech codes directed against hate speech in universities operate to chill traditional Western cultural expression, in that such codes, as read by their academic interpreters, presume that Western culture is itself a deeper manifestation of the vulgar racist and sexist epithet.

BLUE-COLLAR EPITHET VS. LEARNED SMEAR

The new critics argue that racial and sexist epithets are not only based upon false assumptions of fact about race and sexuality but are also (1) devoid of ideational content and (2) emotionally harmful to the victim. Let us take up the assertion that the insult is relatively free of ideational content, hence should not be protected by the First Amendment. The pejorative "Get lost nigger, kike, queer, etc.," is arguably a mere profane grunt, not an idea or opinion. It is also designed to intimidate rather than rationally communicate. Since the grunt is based upon factually false premises about the minority group and is an expression of anger or fear, not a rational idea, why not ban it without fear of compromising the First Amendment? (As we will see, it is not always based on false premises: bigots may hate Jews because of the latter's successes.)

This is an old and venerable position. Spinoza argued for free speech so long as it was based on reason, not "fraud, anger or hatred."[8] This doctrine is not endorsed by the Supreme Court, unless children are the audience.[9] In *Cohen v. California*, the Court held that a jacket bearing the words "Fuck the Draft" was protected by the First Amendment;[10] the Court stated that "one man's vulgarity is another's lyric."[11]

Assume that the reference to "kike" was replaced by something like "you are Jew." From my reading of the New Testament, I have concluded that Jews were responsible for the death of Christ.[12] From my perusal of that great classic, *The Merchant of Venice*, I have concluded that Jews are greedy.[13] From my study of Marx's work on the Jews, I have decided that they are inherently purveyors of the worst excesses of the capitalist system.[14] From my reading of the UN General Assembly resolution passed on November 10, 1975, declaring Zionism "to be a form of racism," I have ascertained that Zionism is indeed racism.[15] From my reading of Richard Wagner[16] and the writer Ludwig Feuerbach,[17] I have determined that Jews are depraved elements in the body politic. Hence, please leave this school or, better yet, leave the country.

The last paragraph is considered but nasty. It is intellectual (in the sense of references to the learned sources) but false in its assertions. It threatens Jews and expresses anger and fear. Do we permit this kind of anti-Semitic statement, because it is clothed in the garments of rational thought, but ban the "Jew is kike" epithet? If we do, it appears that we are expressing a kind of elitist theory of permissible racist speech. Street vernacular won't cut it, but the racism of the academy will.

The "Jew is kike" statement is popular speech based upon a two-thousand-year history of "learned" and elitist anti-Semitism, taught by church fathers, great literary titans, profound musical composers, famous revolutionaries, and learned scholars. It is not "low value" speech (that is, speech that conveys no political message), to use the terminology popularized by some scholars.[18] It expresses a point of view on a public issue, the status of Jews. It is a disgusting opinion. My gut reaction is to ban the popular version as well as the more "learned." But that cannot be done without fatally compromising the First Amendment.

IDEATIONAL AND EMOTIONAL CONTENT OF HATE SPEECH

Discourse in the realms of politics, religion, and law, let alone art or cinema, is often in reality a mixture of metaphor, rhetoric, insult, authority, "common sense," and imagery.[19] It is not a rational, logical exposition in the form mathematicians or scientists use.[20] Indeed, in our secular era it is especially difficult to reach rational consensus on ethical and moral issues. The abortion debate is an example: there is no mathematical or scientific route to an answer; there is no rational or logical method to determine when human life begins. The opposing camps argue by way of imagery and metaphor.

One camp will appeal to the concept of murdering the unborn, the other to the woman's right to control her body. Political discussion usually does not proceed in a linear fashion to some truth. The death penalty presents another example: one side will publish pictures of execution and otherwise argue the barbarity of capital punishment; the opposing camp will appeal to the idea of retribution. Another example is the debate about whether the war in Iraq was just. Professor Arthur Leff has gone so far (much too far, I believe) as to assert on a similar issue that there is no way to "prove" justness or the lack of it except by using a "louder and louder voice," "or by defining it as so."[21] The same is true for the debate between bishops of the Roman Catholic Church and members of the gay community about the church's moral disapprobation of homosexuality. (Do we ban gay epithets on campus but permit the cardinals to continue teaching that homosexuality is sinful?) The debates and discussions continue, sometimes indefinitely, with conclusions decided sometimes by changes in technological and economic structure. For example, it is questionable that rational discussion had a greater impact on womens' attitudes toward sexuality than did the pill.

Criticism of hate speech *because* of its emotional content is weak. Much of so-called intellectual debate is vitriolic, hateful,

and derisive. Any cursory reading of book reviews or com-
mentaries upon other thinkers will reveal the biting, often
vicious, cut and parry of the members of the academy. Intellectuals cringe when reading reviews of their work, and, no
doubt, realize that the victims of their own biting reviews will
suffer emotional harm. In a recent *Commentary* issue, Daniel
C. Dennett, a distinguished philosopher, criticized a piece by
David Berlinski as follows: "I love it: Another hilarious dem-
onstration that you can publish bull__t at will just so long as
you say what an editorial board wants to hear in a style it
favors."[22] In an issue of *The New Republic*, Mickey Kaus re-
viewed William F. Buckley's new book, *Gratitude*.[23] The
cover page read, "Mickey Kaus skewers Wm. F. Buckley, Jr."
In the review Kaus called the book "lazily researched and
sloppily argued."[24] Kaus suggested that a reader, knowing
Buckley was the leading conservative in the United States,
"might conclude that American Conservatism was in a fairly
advanced state of decrepitude."[25]

The New Yorker, in a brief review of the movie *The Miser*,
called it "tiresome, simpleminded, infantile."[26] In the *National Review*'s December 31, 1990, issue, movie reviewer
John Simon called the movie *Reversal of Fortune* "thoroughly
offensive" and found parts of it "ineffably tasteless, almost
sacrilegious."[27] Simon, in the same issue, called the Broadway
musical *Shogun* an "unqualified disaster—a bloated nightmare
of stylistic miscegenation."[28] This is emotional warfare, likely
to inflict serious emotional harm upon the authors, producers,
and performers. Do we ban it?

EMOTIONAL DISTRESS

One of the principal conceptual bases for prohibiting racial
epithets stems from the tort of intentional infliction of severe
emotional distress. The *Restatement (Second) of Torts* defined

the tort as follows: "(1) One who by extreme and outrageous conduct intentionally or recklessly causes severe emotional distress to another."[29] One commentator has observed that the " 'extreme and outrageous conduct' component is, in reality, the entirety of the tort."[30] *The Restatement* defined "outrageous," in part, as a case "in which the recitation of the facts to an average member of the community would arouse his resentment against the actor, and lead him to exclaim, 'Outrageous!' "[31]—an "I know it when I see it" test.

The Supreme Court, in *Hustler Magazine v. Falwell*, had this to say about the word: " 'Outrageousness' in the area of political and social discourse has an inherent subjectivity about it which would allow a jury to impose liability on the basis of the jurors' tastes or views, or perhaps on the basis of their dislike of a particular expression. An 'outrageousness' standard thus runs afoul of our longstanding refusal to allow damages to be awarded because the speech in question may have an adverse emotional impact on the audience."[32]

In a somewhat similar vein, John Stuart Mill stated, "Much might be said on the impossibility of fixing where these supposed bounds are to be placed; for if the test be offense to those whose opinions are attacked, I think experience testifies that this offense is given whenever the attack is telling and powerful, and that every opponent who pushes them hard, and whom they find it difficult to answer, appears to them, if he show any strong feeling on the subject, an intemperate opponent."[33]

"Outrageous," nevertheless, is a fair description of some of the battles in scholarly and political journals. "Outrageous" does not exhaust (but is frequently the mark of) avant garde, original work in the arts and literature, as well as mediocre works straining unsuccessfully to be original. The point of the First Amendment is to protect speech that is outrageous. Speech that is sedate, that is non-controversial, that is somewhere within the confines of traditional convention and morality, seldom needs protection.

C.S. Lewis was a brilliant and talented Oxford don, author of serious works on literature as well as world-famous novels of fantasy for children and the young at heart. He was a passionate, believing Christian. He engaged in a debate with another scholar on the existence of God, on which he had written a serious work. The woman who debated him, Elizabeth Anscombe, destroyed his written work on the existence of God and left him in despair. He was forced to reconsider his life, his meaning, and his work. Fortunately he recovered, although he did not again write philosophical works proving the existence of God. He turned instead to his novels for children. He did not change his convictions on the existence of God, despite her rhetorical and intellectual blitzkrieg.[34] As Jonathan Swift once said, "You cannot reason a person out of something he has not been reasoned into."[35] Obviously no one would charge Anscombe with the tort of emotional harm, although she devastated Lewis with intent and with deliberation. Again, warfare in the academy is permissible, but street language is suspect.

In the end, pure reason, whatever that is, is seldom the method by which minds are changed. The use of rhetoric, metaphor, and imagery are, in contrast, powerful instruments for change.[36] For example, Richard Posner has correctly observed that Holmes's *Lochner* dissent, one of the most influential judicial pieces in American jurisprudence, was a model of rhetoric and imagery, as opposed to reason and the calm marshaling of facts.[37] If the First Amendment is going to turn on relative use of emotion, insult, or injury to sensibilities of listener, the nature of speech will change in the direction of the bland and the mediocre. Judges will be thrust into content and style discrimination, required to weigh the proportion of emotion and derision to the percentage of pure reason.

A fine example of the use of action, emotion, and derision is the cinematic treatment of American fundamentalists. It is no secret that screenwriters and directors have not been overly kind to this minority group, who are forever depicted as ignorant, hypocritical boobs. On the silver screen they are pictured as religious frauds who mouth the words of piety while lusting for money and sex. The pictures wound the fundamentalist; it is clear that the directors intend the injury, and the intellectual content (as in many movies) may be thin. The movies are the pictorial equivalent of the epithet, "Fundamentalists are lying hypocritical frauds." I surmise the new critics of the First Amendment are not proposing the censorship of the cinema. They would argue, I suspect, that racism is without question evil, but anti-fundamentalism is widely and wisely supported in the enlightened culture. It is therefore not emotion, diatribe, or hatred that disqualifies speech, but rather lack of truthfulness. We are back to the arguments considered in Chapter 2. Speech is to be treated in the way commercial speech is now treated by the Court: the government is to have the power to ban false speech or correct misleading speech.

CAUSAL RELATIONSHIP, OR FROM WORDS TO HARM

I personally believe that racist and sexist insults and epithets harm the listener, but I confess I do not know the amount or permanence of the alleged harm with scientific certitude. Social scientists attempt to quantify the harm, but their "science" is notoriously inexact. As pointed out above, much vigorous debate and controversy "harms" the recipient of the verbal attack. If discomfort of the listener is to be the test, however, censorship will always be justified. If in the final analysis harm, as perceived by judge or jury, is the measure

by which we regulate speech, there will be nothing left of the
First Amendment. There will be no difference in the treatment of words as contrasted to deeds. When societies choose
to censor, they do so because of perceived potential for harm
as defined by the interests in positions of power. Speech that
government considers harmless will not be censored, and
there is obviously no need for a First Amendment for that
kind of speech. If we deed to government the power to define
what is harmful and to censor speech that in its opinion will
cause harm, we open the way to government thought-control.
As Judge Easterbrook put it, "[a]ny other answer leaves the
government in control of all of the institutions of culture, the
great censor and director of which thoughts are good for
us."[38]

Judge Learned Hand famously made a similar point many
decades ago, when considering the power of government to
censure radical revolutionaries. He rejected the Holmesian
notion of clear and present danger of harm as a slippery, in-
effective test for the protection of free speech. "For Hand,
predictions about the possible effect of speech, empirically
plausible as they might be, would not do as a legal standard
consistent with the safeguarding of free speech."[39] He did not
trust juries: "Juries won't much regard the difference between
the probable result of the words and the purposes of the ut-
terer."[40] That is, juries, courts, and government will always
find harm when unpopular words are uttered, particularly in
times of fear.[41] He eloquently argued, "I am not wholly in
love with Holmes's test and the reason is this. Once you admit that the matter is one of degree [closeness of words to
harm], while you may put it where it genuinely belongs you
so obviously make it a matter of administration, i.e., you give
to Tomdickandharry, D.J., so much latitude . . . that the jig
is at once up. Besides even their Ineffabilities, the Nine Elder
Statesmen, have not shown themselves wholly immune from
the 'herd instinct' and what seems 'immediate and direct' to-

day may seem very remote next year even though circumstances surrounding the utterance be unchanged."[42]
    In 1947 Norman Cousins, editor of the *Saturday Review
of Literature*, urged that group libel laws be adopted to curb
hate speech, such as Nazi anti-Semitic crusades.[43] Learned
Hand made another powerful argument against censorship of
hate speech:

> It is quite true that the kind of defamation you have
> in mind has that tendency to promote disorder which
> has been the conventional justification for all criminal
> libel; yet, if one thinks through the working of such
> prosecutions in practice, I should suppose that their ef-
> fect would be rather to exacerbate than to assuage the
> feelings which lie behind the defamation of groups. . . .
> The passions which lie at the root of such utterances do
> not have their bases in evidence, and will not yield to it.
> . . . There is no remedy for the evil, but the slow advance
> of the spirit of toleration; and I believe that the sup-
> pression of intolerance always tends to make it more bit-
> ter. This is a result most unsatisfactory to ardent natures
> and it may be wrong; I can only tell you what I believe.[44]

    Beyond all these arguments there is an even more funda-
mental objection to the harm principle (except where imminent physical injury is threatened and likely). Words create
beliefs. Beliefs structure the social and political world. Words
that have bite and significance can harm. Communists, Nazis,
and anti-Semites (Republicans, in the opinion of Democrats,
and vice-versa) can create evil results. But that is why societies
in the past (and present) censor: they want to prevent the evil
that words (as they see them) will create. In every political,
moral, and social conflict of significance, the opposite side will
predict hell and damnation, and sometimes it does so correctly. Thus, the First Amendment is designed to protect
speech that harms; it can have no other purpose. No society

censors, unless and until the powers that be conclude that the speech at issue is harmful. If we measure censorship by the societal harm of the speech, we give to the government the power to determine what is harmful and what can be said. When we move in the direction of measuring regulation of words by their perceived harm, we have gone a long way toward obliterating the distinction between conduct and words in our constitutional scheme. Most governments in the world chill speech because of its perceived, or real, impact; in America we have chosen to take the risk as the price of a free society. This proposition is a cliché, a stock phrase, but not the less true for its banality.

Obviously speech that is too closely brigaded with (simple) violent behavior is not protected. When we attempt to measure the constitutional protection of words by their causal relationship with complex societal harm, we move into dangerous waters. As Judge Easterbrook has said, "Social science studies are very difficult to interpret."[45] He added, "Because much of the effect of speech comes through a process of socialization, it is difficult to measure incremental benefits and injuries caused by particular speech."[46]

Once we begin to censure speech on major issues because of its perceived societal harm, we have rationalized pervasive censorship. For example, censors may allege the following: television violence causes violent behavior; communist speech causes totalitarian overthrow of democratic government; criticism of religion creates a societal breakdown of the nuclear family; deconstructionism is the ruination of literary studies. In all of these and other great disputes, the protagonists, pro and con, of causality are able to quote their favorite social science research papers. However, sociological research is a notoriously inexact science. If we permit legislatures to pass censorship laws based upon such uncertain science, we will in effect justify a weak rational-basis test for the validity of such legislation. That is, a statute will pass muster if the legislature has a fairly reasonable empirical basis for the censorship. Such a test is not much different from that for the validity of legislation regulating conduct. The First Amendment will be a much-weakened doctrine.

DIRECT INSULTS VERSUS PUBLIC ASSAULT

At this juncture I should examine another issue. Above, I discussed the tort of intentional infliction of emotional distress. That doctrine can serve as a basis for statutes forbidding racist and sexist speech. I discussed some objections to such a use. But should we distinguish the infliction of emotional harm on private figures from the infliction of such harm on public figures, or from racist remarks not directed at any individual? The difference, for example, is between the hate speech directed at an individual and generalized hate speech set forth in a book. Another difference is between hate speech directed at a private person and that directed at a public, political figure.

The *Hustler Magazine v. Falwell* Court considered an item in a magazine in which Falwell was depicted as having a drunken, incestuous encounter with his mother. The story was labeled a parody. The Court held that *public figures and public officials* may not recover for the tort of intentional infliction of emotional distress by reason of such publications as the one then at issue without showing in addition that the publication contains a false statement of fact which was made with " 'actual malice,' i.e., with knowledge that the statement was false or with reckless disregard as to whether or not it was true." That is, defamation is actionable, but not emotional, attack. "This is not merely a 'blind application' of the *New York Times* standard. . . . It reflects our considered judgment that such a standard is necessary to give adequate 'breathing space' to the freedoms protected by the First Amendment."[47]

In the facts as presented to the Court there was no false statement of fact, since the story was an obvious satire;[48] it was deliberate and mean-spirited, but protected.

The Court's reasoning, arguably, is that the core meaning of the First Amendment is to protect public political debate. When private figures are involved, the balance shifts to protection of emotional health, in the case of racist or sexist speech. This position permits a racial epithet in a magazine or book directed at a public figure, not a private individual. This position would also imply the protection of racial epithets aimed at no one in particular (e.g., assertions in a book about racial inferiority of x group) as distinguished from one directed at a particular private party. The former case would not involve infliction of emotional distress against a particular individual, and it would be closer to a generalized political statement than an insult. The *Hustler* opinion does not necessarily permit a face-to-face insult of a public figure. Arguably, such an exchange could evoke a fighting-words rationale, i.e., an impermissible invitation to a fight. Justice White, concurring in the *R.A.V.* case, distinguished between face-to-face insult and, for example, "[b]urning a cross at a political rally."[49] The latter, he asserted, would be protected.[50]

I have the following problems with private-vs.-public distinctions in the area of allegedly racist or sexist speech. First, it is an opening wedge to permitting excessive state regulation of private speech. That is a potentially momentous intrusion. If the state can regulate the civility of private discourse in matters of race or sex, there is no rational reason for preventing the state from requiring defined civility across the entire range of private conversation and speech—and the definer will be the state. My examples of literary and scholarly savagery toward opponents is an example of the kind of discourse that could be regulated under cover of diminishing emotional harm and softening the edge of argument. A characteristic of totalitarian societies has been the state's often successful effort to censor and chill private speech.

Second, private speech is essential to the democratic process. Citizens form and reform their attitudes to local economic, social, and financial issues by the stuff and substance of their private gossip and discourse. It is artificial to separate the two and permit censorship of the private speech. It is dangerous if we do it under the guise of chilling the infliction of emotional harm in an outrageous form. It would directly reach content that offends, but regulation of offensive speech threatens to reduce speech to syrupy irrelevance and blandness.

Third, it is impossible to limit the ban to statements only of the nature of "*X*, you are a kike." People differ radically in their definitions of what is racist or sexist. Indeed the terms are used sometimes with careless abandon. To some, for example, the advocacy of anti-quota policies is racist, and in the context of a private argument, a racist epithet. In the domain of private speech, the courts would enter a thicket of the usual interpretation and development that would inevitably act as a chill and deterrent to face-to-face, private speech.

Fourth, private speech has been transformed in recent years. The use of four-letter words has exploded. Also, the distinction between women and men in the use of profanity has largely vanished. The differences between the sexes on this score are a thing of the past. The cinema, which reflects the popular culture, every day shows the use by men and women of words like "fuck" that were unmentionable in polite society a few decades ago. In a sense, the effort by some to censor epithets is an effort to restore in modern fashion an old morality.

Fifth, the banning of one-on-one insult is a throwback to

the disreputable fighting-words doctrine—that is, the doctrine permitting censorship of words that will lead to a brawl. This approach would permit the censorship of insulting words, because they create emotional hurt or lead to violence. But this is to reward a kind of macho, barroom mentality. The speaker is hostage to the thin-skinned listener: if the latter tends to weep, or alternatively, to respond with fists, the remarks can be censored. Where a pugnacious John Wayne listens, yes to censorship; if Wayne doesn't give a damn and is inclined to a pacific response, no censorship. If a woman is the target, she may be less inclined to belt the verbal assaulter. This creates the possibility of a sexist distinction: men as targets, fighting speech; women as targets, non-actionable verbal insult. This is dangerous. We have already pointed out that the essence of free speech principles is to permit words that offend. Otherwise the First Amendment is emasculated, since no one ever worries about benign speech. As for the violent-reaction component, this operates to constitutionalize the censoriousness of the most violent of our listeners.

Perhaps most important is another point, however. The argument that racist speech directed at a private individual is more deserving of censorship than that directed at the world in general is based on a dangerous premise. It supposes that the private epithet creates more harm than a published racist philosophical tract. This proposition is empirically dubious. Television broadcasts or books aimed at creating general racist sentiments against a group or a class are more dangerous to society than the personal insult. The latter hurts an individual, but the former can influence vast groups, mold public opinion, and create a racist environment. Of course, this merely reflects the truism that books and television have consequences, which is why, absent the First Amendment, society always attempts to censor what it considers dangerous speech. But this discussion underlines the danger of using harm as an argument for limiting speech: the end result is pervasive censorship. Of course, physical harm, the proximity of words to immediate violence, is another matter and properly to be regulated.

Defamation and Hate Speech

We can profit from a discussion of defamation, a category of speech that, when factually false, may not be legally protected. Many experts believe that defamation actions intimidate the press. The *New York Times v. Sullivan*[51] standard for public figures, requiring proof of actual malice, falsity, and harm to reputation, was intended to preserve a vigorous and feisty press. In recent years, plaintiffs with deep pockets or attorneys on contingent fees have, it has been argued, succeeded in intimidating the press.[52] Even the possibility of suit sometimes causes publishers and novelists to alter their copy. Professor Laurence H. Tribe has observed that since the unanimous *Sullivan* decision, "[T]he Court has become deeply fragmented about almost every respect of libel, and the doctrine has become a frustrating tangle for all concerned—a mysterious labyrinth for those seeking to clear their names and a costly and unpredictable burden for the speakers the first amendment is designed to protect."[53]

There is a similarity between defamation and racist and sexist speech. Defamation is directed at a specific person.[54] The same is true for much, but certainly not all, racist speech. The defamatory speech (to be actionable) must assert a false fact and harm the reputation of an individual. It differs from racist speech in that racist speech is sometimes true, in the perverted sense that when someone says, "I hate you, wealthy kike," the emotion is genuine and the victim is indeed a Jew, and may be wealthy. The emotion is a reaction of bigoted envy of the object's success. In addition, the harm is not necessarily in damage to reputation (although it may be that, too) but in fear and intimidation. However, there is very frequently an element of falseness, in that the ethnic slur is based upon a flawed and false view of the racial or gender group. Sometimes the slur is based, however, on hatred of the truth, e.g., the financial prowess of certain Jews or Asians.

Defamation of a group is probably not a valid cause of action anymore.[55] In a sense, sexist and racist speech is an offshoot of group libel. The epithet "X is a kike" flows from the general proposition that Jews are all kikes (Ugh! says the bigot), hence X, a Jew, is a hated kike. The critics of traditional free speech doctrine would like to reintroduce the group defamation concept.

Discourse on public figures is the stuff of political speech. Some speech is general, such as debate over the value of private property and over the redistribution of wealth. But in the case of politics, most debate necessarily also involves criticism of individual political actors: Richard Nixon was or was not a crook; the "Keating Five" were or were not beholden to savings and loan largess;[56] Senator John Tower was or was not an alcoholic.[57] If there were doubts, the Ariel Sharon and General William Westmoreland trials demonstrated the inextricable linkage between biting critique of individual public figures and the stuff of political debate.[58] The Westmoreland trial involved the country's fundamental differences over the wisdom and conduct of the Vietnam War. The Sharon trial touched the deep divisions over Israel's conduct of the Lebanese invasion. Defamation doctrine, in effect, subjects much of political speech to the test of truthfulness (plus, of course, the chastening *New York Times v. Sullivan* requirement of actual malice). Justices Hugo Black, Arthur Goldberg, and William Douglas concurred in that case, arguing that the First Amendment required absolute immunity for criticisms of public officials, not the actual malice standard.[59] Actual malice "is knowledge that [the statement published] was false or (made) with reckless disregard of whether it was false or not."[60] The Westmoreland and Sharon trials reinforced the strength of Justices Black, Douglas, and Goldberg's arguments. Both Westmoreland and Sharon were powerful public figures who had clear access to the press to argue their causes and to cleanse their names. They did not need the libel process.

When the object of alleged defamation is a private party, there is no First Amendment requirement of actual malice.[61] The absence of public or official status tips the scales in the direction of preserving private reputation.[62] However, the First Amendment still requires the plaintiff to show some fault on the part of the defendant.[63] Where no public figure is involved and the matter is private, less First Amendment protection is available. However, in such a case the First Amendment interest in vigorous truthful debate would preserve the defense of truth against a defamation charge and would probably require some fault upon the part of the defendant who uttered a false and defamatory statement. The Court's distinctions between private and public figures and between private and public concerns have been widely criticized as a confusing labyrinth. For example, Professor Tribe stated that the "latest accommodation between the First Amendment and the individual's occupational interests lacks coherence."[64] He also pointed out that individuals have been suing authors of novels and films with increasing frequency for allegedly depicting them in a false and harmful way. This trend has chilled the creative expression of authors and publishers."[65]

In the case of private, social talk, much speech is gossip about the foibles of our friends and neighbors: next-door neighbor Paul is or is not an alcoholic. If we are to be held at risk in such speech, as indeed we are, it is only the relative litigation-adverseness of the potential plaintiffs that saves us. Who could pass a day safely if speech were actually held to the litmus test of truth to which it is subject in theory? We could not utter a word without verification and audit. Imagine the following scene at a party:

"What do you think of Harry?"

"I cannot talk about Harry unless and until I research the truthfulness of the gossip in which I was about to engage."

Defamation is, on reflection, a less than perfect doctrine (although an old and venerable one) that is workable to date only because of the relative lack of litigation. In that sense, the doctrine is much like anti-adultery laws, endurable only so long as not extensively enforced.

The end result is that much political speech, which is often about individual politicians, is governed by a truth test subject to the actual-malice criteria. The truth test also applies to private speech, except that the permissible state standard for plaintiffs to prove is probably negligence. Therefore, a truth test strikes deep in the heart even of speech that lies at the core of protected speech. With that wedge in place, the new critics can argue more effectively for a similar test for racist and sexist speech aimed at a specific person (or at groups, if that person can get group libel reestablished as good doctrine).

The contention may be met by the objection that the defamation doctrine is widely criticized and that, in the opinions of many learned commentators, the *Sullivan* test, even with the malice standard, is not working well. Nevertheless, once one accepts truth as a valid First Amendment criteria (as it is accepted in defamation) the breach is apparent and difficult to contain doctrinally—that is, as a matter of the usual legal arguments by way of analogy from one case and body of law to the next. That difficulty is what I pointed out in Chapter 2 on truth-seeking, slippery slopes, and the First Amendment.

FACT AND OPINION

A fact-versus-opinion issue lurks here. Defamation turns on the truthfulness of asserted fact, not opinion. "Under the First Amendment [in defamation actions, and arguably beyond] there is no such thing as a false idea. . . . But there is no constitutional value in false statements of fact."[66] Thus, opinions are protected, though a recent Court opinion has perhaps fuzzed the distinction between fact and opinion by stating that opinions that are in reality implied assertions of false facts will be treated as statements of erroneous fact.[67]

Nevertheless, the judicial distinction between fact and opinion still holds in general. The new critics of traditional First Amendment doctrine argue that hate and sexist speech is a species of false fact. Since false facts have no constitutional value in defamation doctrine (or arguably, under any doctrine), they will contend that such speech should receive no constitutional protection. Traditional civil libertarians will argue that sexist and racist talk is (even if analogized to defamation) in reality protected (if nasty) opinion, not assertion of fact; indeed, it is opinion that has proven remarkably resistant to facts about the religious or racial group. The very ability and success of certain groups may lead a less successful group to hate and despise them. That is, positive facts about a given group may form the basis for prejudice; for example, Jews and Asians may be at the top of the economic or academic ladder. The hatred may also be the product of fear, anger, or envy disconnected from reason and fact: "You are different, and therefore I hate you." All of these differences may be true in fact.

The distinction between fact and opinion is tricky, because of the ambiguity and uncertainty of so-called "facts" and the value and clarity of many so-called "opinions." History is replete with the canonization of "facts" that on further research, debate in the free market of discourse, and study turn out to be fictions. Newton's Laws, once considered the infallible keys to the universe, turned out in light of relativity theory to be of limited application. Historical "truths" become falsehoods as each new generation reinterprets history in the light of current wisdom.

This progress of truth to falsehood and back again (witness the varying reputations of Christopher Columbus over the decades as minority groups in American society gained power) is a sample of the pragmatic "principle" in action. Truth is measured, so to speak, by a process of dialogue and experiment, reaching temporary consensus only to be changed or abandoned as the political, cultural, and scientific dialogue continues. A belief is a rather weak consensus, compared to its more vigorous sibling, the fact, which is a judgment that has reached a firmer consensus in the language game. But there is no necessary, clear dividing line; we often speak of a continuum, in which certain assertions are more probable than others.

The Court, in finding it necessary to distinguish (hard and fast) between fact and opinion has unwittingly entered into a kind of judicial "pop philosophy." Ancient philosophers, such as Plato (and some more recent), viewed truth as some ideal form or reality out there that human Reason would perceive or possess. Lesser degrees of being or becoming were mere opinion or spurious rhetoric. Later philosophers continually theorized about the nature of knowledge as contrasted with belief or conjecture. Is a fact something that Jones states with great confidence? Is an opinion something he is more diffident about? Is a fact something about which a jury lacks reasonable doubt? Is an opinion something that is reached in court by a preponderance of the evidence, something short of the reasonable doubt standard? But since when is subjective confidence a measure of the truth? Are there measures of verification that all will accept? And why is universal concurrence (if such there be) proof of fact, rather than opinion? Was Newton's gravitational theory a fact? It has since been replaced by relativity theory. And so on, and so on.

Some modern philosophers, such as Derrida, have adopted a skeptical—some would say a nihilistic—approach to the search for objective truth. He and his colleagues argue that everything is interpretation. The author is unimportant, and the text is not available as some objective datum but instead is subject to (indeed created by) the interpretation of the reader. In this approach, the texts subject to the deconstructive engine are not only literary works but history as well. Other thinkers in a similar vein, argue that historical and social truths are constructs of whatever class is in power, such as white males. Many modern philosophers view much (if not all) that passes as alleged objective fact as being in reality socially created or contextualized "opinion."[68] Philosophers and scientists who do not buy into this approach still recognize that even "hard" science, e.g., physics, is legitimately the subject of debate, conjecture, uncertainty, and frequent revision. In any event, the definitions of knowledge and truth, the nature of reality, and the issue of whether there is a reality outside of human relationships, language, and experimentation have been the stuff of millenia of philosophical debate. The Court, however, driven by the necessities of defamation doctrine, takes it upon itself to "solve" (butcher?) the complex philosophical disputes since it must make hard and fast distinctions between so-called opinion and fact. This is an impossible task, except in the simplest of "fact" situations. As a result, the Court chills debate by its adherence to a highly debatable and oversimplified philosophical notion of truth.

Consider this example. The Supreme Court has characterized the following kind of statement as an assertion of fact: "In my opinion John Jones is a liar."[69] The Court asserted that the opinion is predicated on "facts" that can be proven or disproven. However, the Court gave as an example of protected opinion the statement (which I paraphrase), "In my opinion Mayor Jones is an ignoramus because he accepts the teachings of Marx and Lenin."[70] Yet surely (we can argue), the bloody history of Leninism in the twentieth century proves the mayor a fool as well as an ignoramus. Is the evil of Leninism a fact or an opinion? Many would argue that it is a "fact" more obvious than even the simplest of "You are a liar" statements.

My point in mentioning these Supreme Court examples is to show (fairly easily, I believe) how tricky is the fact/opinion distinction. Perhaps very simple "facts" are indeed easy to deal with. For example, "Jones is a liar; he said he is eighteen but he is in reality seventy-six." (However, Jones may have meant, "In my heart I feel eighteen!") We check the birth certificate and ask him to show his wrinkles.

I am not asserting by all this that I believe in a kind of skeptical nihilism about the existence of "facts." The earth is round, not flat; relativity is valid; the Holocaust occurred, and revisionism is in error; etc., etc. However, across a vast area of the most important discourse there is controversy and doubt about this or that alleged fact. Circumstances give different statements a certain probability of validity. Reasonable people can doubt the probability judgments of other reasonable persons. (Who is reasonable, however, is not so easy to determine.) This goes on all the time. As Wittgenstein puts it in his proposition 335: "The procedure in a court of law rests on the fact that circumstances give statements a certain probability."[71] These conclusions as to probability vary with time and discussion. Again, as Wittgenstein argues in his proposition 336: "But what men consider reasonable or unreasonable alters. At certain periods men find reasonable what at other periods they found unreasonable. And vice versa."[72]

Wittgenstein argues that at the core of every language game is a nest of unshakable assumptions. For example, the earth was here a few years ago; this is, indeed, my hand; I have or had two parents. We operate in a nest of fundamental assumptions that are the foundation of our language game.[73] It is senseless to doubt them; doubt has no meaning in that regard. They are the "hinges"[74] of our language game. It is meaningless to doubt that this is my hand. I cannot make a mistake in that sense; if indeed it is not my hand, my entire universe collapses, or I am mad. But beyond that are multitudes of assertions that we can meaningfully doubt and test, because we do operate in a language game with certain core assumptions that are meaningless to doubt. These are propositions that, when established, we believe. Wittgenstein asserts in proposition 177: "What I know, I believe."[75] In this context, the ordinary domain of debate and discussion involves propositions with varying degrees of probable accuracy; belief and fact are part of a continuum.

The fact/opinion distinction is clearly a powerful support for critics of traditional liberal support of the First Amendment. The Supreme Court has asserted in defamation cases that false facts, even when couched as opinions, have no First Amendment value. Hate speech and sexist speech is categorized by such critics as false fact and hence, in their opinion, subject to extensive government censorship. They can argue that the Supreme Court should permit censorship of "false facts" in the domain of general political and social debate not involving traditional defamation or obscenity. Therefore, hate and sexist speech should be regulatable. I believe, for reasons given in this and the past chapter, that the result would be catastrophic. This approach would permit Congress to establish a political equivalent of the Securities and Exchange Commission (the "Political Truth Commission") to regulate the truth value of political debate. Given the murky distinctions between fact and opinion, this would amount to a general license for litigators to convince courts to establish a sweeping censorship of unpopular ideas.

A healthy First Amendment should protect (in non-defamation, non–commercial speech areas) the publication or utterance of allegedly false fact as well as allegedly false opinion, since the distinction between the two is sometimes temporary and frequently elusive. Freeze the discussion, and liberty is curtailed. Whether some fact is indeed a fact is frequently at the heart of most significant debate; if we give courts the general power to chill debate by determining what is a fact, we give them too much power. The fact that they have that power in the area of defamation illustrates the disturbing significance of defamation as a qualified exception to the general protections of the First Amendment.

Education and Hate Speech

Despite what I have said, I agree that American society, in the school context, does work on the basis that certain opinions and ideas have been validated. Absent that, there could be no coherent public secondary school curriculum. Particularly in the hard sciences, this is a workable proposition. We permit advocacy of the "flat earth" science outside the classroom, but not in it. We make a pragmatic judgment that accepted bodies of knowledge should be taught in the schools. Free speech principles apply to protect soapbox, magazine, or newspaper advocacy of contrary views, such as creationism, *outside* the classroom. This is a safety valve for dissent. (Obviously, creationists disagree with this limitation.)

However, if we are not careful, the school system can indoctrinate students with the prevailing orthodoxy.[76] I agree that without some professional control over the curriculum, school would degenerate into chaos and propaganda rather than education.[77] I refer in particular to the secondary classroom, where the students are young children. The issues get trickier at the college level, where students are young adults and diversity in teaching, no matter how "heretical," should be permitted. Yet even there I admit the need for standards; the physics professor who teaches the Ptolemaic system as correct should be fired. (Needless to say, however, even in physics there are vast areas of debate, disagreement, and imaginative uses of theory and speculation.) The issues get even trickier with teaching varieties of political and aesthetic theory. In these fields it is much more difficult to reach a consensus, no matter how defined.

The danger is that school authorities may use the curriculum to impose on students orthodoxies that are political rather than neutral, scientific principles. (Even in science, as we have often noted, there is ample room for debate, contention, and ambiguity.) Lately, on many campuses politically correct thinking—not merely hard, scientific correctness—has been enforced, only one species of which is the attempted banning of racist and sexist epithets in or outside the classroom.[78] Faculty on many campuses have attempted to eliminate the "grand prejudice"[79] that Western culture and civilization should occupy the center of education. Where the university is a state institution, the First Amendment makes this kind of indoctrination, which involves the censorship of dissenting professors, a legal as well as moral and cultural issue.

The reference to the "grand prejudice" illustrates the point made earlier about the impossibility of cabining areas of alleged certainty from realms of uncertainty. I believe there is a fairly wide consensus that sexual and racist epithets are false and grotesque modes of speech; it is impossible, however, to contain censorship directed at the epithet once we grant the validity of such censorship. The university community appears to be moving toward wide agreement that racial and sexist epithets are merely shallow forms of deeper prejudice, notably the "illusion" that Western civilization and certain "dead white males," such as John Locke, are valuable or worthy. The argument is that the pillars of Western thought, such as Jefferson, Aristotle, and Shakespeare, rationalized racism, sexism, and imperialism (depending on the illustrious figure involved) and are the causes of today's alleged Western racism and sexism. Hence they must be dismissed from the academy, or at least minimized. In short, many in the university community seem to be arguing that Western civilization is the intellectual cause of Western racism and sexism. Molefi Asante, chair of African-American studies at Temple University, has argued for an Afrocentric curriculum, premised on the works of ancient African scholars.[80] "There are only two positions," he says. "Either you support multiculturalism in American education, or you support the maintenance of white supremacy."[81]

The advocates of multiculturalism and politically correct thinking on campus argue that all knowledge is suspect, since it flows from power and white domination. In order to avoid the charge that their position is equally suspect, they make an exception for their lessons on race and ethnicity: Truth *does* reside, they assert, in their propositions about the debilitating role of white power. Power in the hands of certified minorities is correct. Thus, for example, since Shakespeare was, as they see it, sexist and imperialist, his work is of no importance, except perhaps to make conspicuous the elements of white power in the so-called academic liberal-arts canon. This is a position espoused by self-described left-wingers.

But Marxists do not necessarily espouse such extremism. As Irving Howe, himself a prominent leftist, wrote recently, "George Lukacs, the most influential Marxist critic of the twentieth century," wrote that, " 'those who do not know Marxism may be surprised at the respect for the *classical heritage of mankind* which one finds in the really great representatives of that doctrine.' "[82] Howe also quotes Leon Trotsky to the effect that:

> If I say that the importance of *The Divine Comedy* lies in the fact that it gives me an understanding of the state of mind of certain classes in a certain epoch, this means that I transform it into *a mere historical document*. . . . How is it thinkable that there should be not a historical but a *directly aesthetic relationship* between us and a medieval Italian book? This is explained by the fact that in a class society, in spite of its changeability, there are cer-

tain common features. Works of art developed in a medieval Italian city can affect us too. What does this require? . . . That these feelings and moods shall have received such broad, intense, powerful expressions as to have raised them above the limitations of the life of those days.[83]

Some conservative followers of the law and economics movement, including interest group theory, make much the same charge as the multiculturalists. For example, some have argued that political pressure and interest-group politics explain the scope of First Amendment doctrine.[84] They deny that ideas have power, at least in comparison to the power of economic interest. Hence, in the area of the commercial speech doctrine they attempt to demonstrate that the Constitution, the courts, and the lawyers all mold First Amendment doctrine in response to the economic power of corporate elites.

Needless to say, if legislators and judges begin to agree that white power underlies the supposed majesty of the First Amendment as well as of the liberal arts canon, they will be tempted to uphold censorship in state-run campuses to eliminate the influence of Plato, Aristotle, Locke, and the other "dead white males." At the least, they will begin to accept the validity of arguments that the First Amendment does not necessarily bar censorship of the "grand prejudice" if "proof" can be adduced that Western civilization embraces false values. Such evidence will become an accepted matter of proof in litigation upon this subject. Censorship will be canonized as a morally correct and historically valid method of teaching the truth.

NOTES

1. *See e.g.*, Richard Delgado, *Campus Antiracism Rules: Constitutional Narratives in Collision*, 85 Nw. U.L. Rev. 343 (1991)

[hereinafter Delgado *Campus Antiracism*]; Richard Delgado, *Words That Wound: A Tort Action for Racial Insults, Epithets, and Name-Calling*, 17 Harv. C.R.-C.L. L. Rev. 133 (1982); Marjorie Heins, *Banning Words: A Comment on "Words That Wound"*, 18 Harv. C.R.-C.L. L. Rev. 585 (1983); Richard Delgado, *Professor Delgado Replies*, 18 Harv. C.R.-C.L. L. Rev. 592 (1983); Steve France, *Hate Goes to College*, 76 A.B.A. J., July 1990, at 44; Kent Greenawalt, *Insults and Epithets: Are They Protected Speech?*, 42 Rutgers L. Rev. 287 (1990); David Kretzmer, *Freedom of Speech and Racism*, 8 Cardozo L. Rev. 445 (1987); Charles R. Lawrence, *If He Hollers Let Him Go: Regulating Racist Speech on Campus*, Duke L.J. 431 (1990); Mari J. Matsuda, *Public Response to Racist Speech: Considering the Victim's Story*, 87 Mich. L. Rev. 2320 (1989); Rodney A. Smolla, Symposium, *Free Speech and Religious, Racial and Sexual Harassment*, 32 Wm. & Mary L. Rev. 207 (1991); Symposium, *Language as Violence v. Freedom of Expression: Canadian and American Perspectives on Group Defamation*, 37 Buffalo L. Rev. 337 (1989); Symposium, *Offensive and Libelous Speech*, 47 Wash. & Lee L. Rev. 1 (1990).

2. Numerous colleges and universities have enacted student conduct codes or modified old ones to chill such speech or similar speech. State universities are subject to First Amendment scrutiny. A number of federal courts have held state university codes to be in violation of the First Amendment. *See e.g.*, Doe v. University of Michigan, 720 F. Supp. 852 (E.D. Mich. 1989).

3. *See, e.g.*, Heins, *supra* note 1.

4. Chaplinsky v. New Hampshire, 315 U.S. 568, 572 (1942). Professor Gunther points out, "Significantly however, the Court has not sustained a conviction on the basis of the fighting words doctrine since Chaplinsky." Gerald Gunther, *Individual Rights in Constitutional Law* 744 (5th ed. 1992).

5. Roth v. United States, 354 U.S. 476, 485 (1957).

6. New York Times v. Sullivan, 376 U.S. 254, 268 (1964).

7. See Nicholas Wolfson, *Corporate First Amendment Rights and the SEC* 63–6 (1990).

8. Benedict Spinoza, *Theological-Political Treatise, in* The Chief Works of Benedict Spinoza, 258 (R.H.M. Elwes, trans., 1883).

9. The Supreme Court in FCC v. Pacifica Foundation, 438

U.S. 726 (1978) permitted censorship of vulgar words on radio during hours in which children were likely to be in the audience.

10. 403 U.S. 15 (1971).

11. *Id.* at 25.

12. *See* Lucy Davidowicz, *How They Teach the Holocaust*, 90 Commentary, Dec. 1990, at 25, 27.

13. William Shakespeare, *The Merchant of Venice.* For a discussion of the complexities of the play, see Allan Bloom, *Giants and Dwarfs* 64–82 (1990).

14. Karl Marx, *On the Jewish Question* (1844).

15. Jeane J. Kirkpatrick, *How the PLO Was Legitimized*, 88 Commentary, July 1989. The resolution was later withdrawn.

16. Jacob Katz, *The Darker Side of Genius: Richard Wagner's Anti-Semitism* (1986).

17. Michael A. Meyer, *Anti-Semitism and Jewish Identity*, 88 Commentary, Nov. 1989, at 35, 37.

18. *See, e.g.*, Cass R. Sunstein, *Pornography and the First Amendment*, 1986 Duke L.J. 589; Larry Alexander, *Low Value Speech*, 83 Nw. U.L. Rev. 547 (1989); Cass R. Sunstein, *Low Value Speech Revisited*, 83 Nw. U.L. Rev. 555 (1989).

19. *See* Richard Posner, *Law and Literature: A Misunderstood Relation* 281–7 (1989).

20. *See* Richard Posner, *The Problems of Jurisprudence*, 148–53 (1990).

21. Arthur Leff, *Economic Analysis of Law: Some Realism about Nominalism*, 60 Va. L. Rev. 451, 454 (1974).

22. Daniel C. Dennett, *Denying Darwin, David Berlinski, and Critics*, 102 Commentary, Sept. 1996, at 6.

23. Mickey Kaus, *Mickey Kaus Skewers Wm. F. Buckley*, The New Republic, Dec. 31, 1990, at 34.

24. *Id.* at 34.

25. *Id.*

26. *Goings On About Town: The Theatre*, The New Yorker, (Nov. 19, 1990), at 4.

27. John Simon, *Odd Couples*, 42 National Review, Dec. 31, 1990, at 46.

28. *Id.* at 49.

29. *Restatement (Second) of Torts* § 46 (1965).

30. David Givelber, *The Right to Minimum Social Decency and the Limits of Evenhandedness: Intentional Infliction of Emotional Distress by Outrageous Conduct*, 82 Colum. L. Rev. 42, 46 (1982).

31. Restatement (Second) of Torts § 46 cmt. d (1965).

32. Hustler Magazine v. Falwell 485 U.S. 46, 55 (1988). The Court admitted limitations in the doctrine. "We recognized in *Pacifica Foundation* that speech that is 'vulgar,' 'offensive,' and 'shocking' is 'not entitled to absolute protection under all circumstances.'" *Id.* at 56 (quoting FCC v. Pacifica Found., 438 U.S. 726, 747 [1978]).

33. John Stuart Mill, *On Liberty* 51 (D. Spitz, ed., 1975).

34. A. N. Wilson, *Biography of C.S. Lewis* 213–5, 220 (1990). Wilson wrote that Elizabeth Anscombe, Lewis's opponent, "was quite equal to the bullying and the exploitation of the audience to which Lewis resorted." *Id.* at 213.

35. Posner, *The Problems of Jurisprudence, supra* note 20, at 151.

36. *Id.* at 150.

37. *Id.* at 394–5 (citing Lochner v. New York, 198 U.S. 45 [1905]).

38. American Bookseller Ass'n, Inc. v. Hudnut, 771 F.2d 323, 330 (7th Cir. 1985), *aff'd*, 106 S. Ct. 1172 (1986) (mem.).

39. Gerald Gunther, *Learned Hand the Man and the Judge* 158 (1994).

40. *Id.* at 165 (quoting L. Hand in a letter to Oliver Wendell Holmes [late March 1919] Holmes Papers, Harvard Law School.

41. *Id.*

42. *Id.* at 169.

43. *Id.* at 576.

44. *Id.* at 576–7, quoting L. Hand letter in *Saturday Review of Literature*, Feb. 1, 1947, 20.

45. American Booksellers Ass'n v. Hudnut, 771 F.2d 323, n.2 (7th Cir. 1985) *aff'd*, 106 S. Ct. 1172 (1986) (mem.).

46. *Id.*

47. Hustler Magazine v. Falwell, 485 U.S. 46, 56 (1988) (emphasis added).

48. *Id.* at 57.

49. *R.A.V. v. St. Paul*, 505 U.S. 377 (1992).

50. *Id.*

51. New York Times v. Sullivan, 376 U.S. 254 (1964).

52. *See* L. G. Forer, *A Chilling Effect: The Mounting Threat of Libel and Invasion of Privacy Actions to the First Amendment* (1987).

53. Laurence H. Tribe, *American Constitutional Law* 865 (2d ed. 1988).

54. *Id.* at 861–86.

55. In *Beauharnais v. Illinois*, the Court held in a closely decided opinion that defamation of groups was a valid cause of action. 343 U.S. 250 (1952). Tribe, in his authoritative treatise, states that "the continuing validity of the *Beauharnais* holding is very much an open question." *Tribe, supra* note 53, at 861 n. 2.

56. *See* Richard Berke, *Ethics Unit Singles Out Cranston, Chides 4 Others in S & L Inquiry*, N.Y. Times, Feb. 28, 1991, at 1.

57. *See* John Tower, *Consequences: A Personal and Political Memoir* (1991).

58. *See* Forer, *supra* note 52, at 22–3. *See also* Tribe, *supra* note 53, at 869–70 n. 54.

59. New York Times v. Sullivan, 376 U.S. 254, 293 (Black, J., joined by Douglas, J., concurring); *Id.* at 297 (Goldberg, J., joined by Douglas, J., concurring).

60. *Id.* at 280.

61. *See* Dun & Bradstreet, Inc. v. Greenmoss Builders, Inc. 472 U.S. 749 (1985); Gertz v. Robert Welch, Inc. 418 U.S. 323 (1974).

62. *See* Tribe, *supra* note 53, at 873–86.

63. *Id.* at 882.

64. *Id.* at 886.

65. *Id.* at 886 n. 84.

66. Gertz v. Robert Welch, Inc., 418 U.S. 323, 339–40 (1974) (citations omitted).

67. Milkovich v. Lorain Journal Co., 110 S. Ct. 2695 (1990).

68. *See e.g.*, Jacques Derrida, *Of Grammatology* (Gayatri Chakravorty, trans., 1976).

69. Milkovich v. Lorain Journal Co., 497 U.S. 1, 18–9 (1990).

70. *Id.* at 20.

71. Ludwig Wittgenstein, *On Certainty* 42e (G.E.M. Anscombe and G.H. von Wright, eds., 1969).

72. *Id* at 43e.

73. *Id.* at 52e.

74. *Id.* at 341, 44e.

75. *Id.* at 25e.

76. *See Race on Campus*, The New Republic, Feb. 18, 1991, at 5–6, 18–47, 49–53 [hereinafter *Race*].

77. In *Bethel School District No. 403 v. Fraser*, the Court upheld the disciplining of a high school student for "offensive" speech. 478 U.S. 675, 678 (1986). The Court stated, "[S]chools must teach by example the shared values of a civilized social order. . . ." *Id.* at 683. *See also* Hazelwood School Dist. v. Kuhlmeier, 484 U.S. 260, 271–2 (1988). For a summary of the cases affirming Supreme Court protection of traditional First Amendment rights of state university students, see David Rosenberg, Note, *Racist Speech, the First Amendment, and Public Universities: Taking a Stand on Neutrality*, 76 Cornell L. Rev. 549, 564–69 (1991).

78. *See, e.g.*, France, *supra* note 1, at 44; *Race, supra* note 76; Ed Gallucci, *A Gathering Storm over the Politically Correct*, Newsweek, Dec. 24, 1990, at 48; *Academic Groups Fighting the "Politically Correct Left" Gain Momentum*, Chron. of Higher Educ., Dec. 12, 1990 at A-3; Anne Matthews, *Deciphering Victorian Underwear and Other Seminars*, N.Y.Times, Feb. 10, 1991 (Magazine), at 42; John Searle, *The Battle over the University*, N.Y. Rev. of Books, Dec. 6, 1990, at 34; *Speech Codes and Free Speech*, Boston Globe, Feb. 26, 1991 (Editorial), at 14; *"The Storm over the University": An Exchange*, N.Y. Rev. of Books, Feb. 14, 1991, at 48.

79. Gallucci, *supra* note 78, at 48.

80. *Id.* at 54.

81. *Id.*

82. *Race, supra* note 76, at 41. (Emphasis added.)

83. *Id.* at 41. (Emphasis added.)

84. Fred S. McChesney, *A Positive Regulatory Theory of the First Amendment*, 20 Conn. L. Rev. 355 (1988).

CHAPTER 4

INEQUALITY

The modern critics of traditional First Amendment jurisprudence argue powerfully that subjugated groups are incapable of relying successfully on free speech. This is a doctrine that belittles speech as an important basis of free society. It views power relationships in economics, race, or gender as fundamental structures that condition, limit, or systemically distort speech. Hence, speech is derivative, coercive, or manipulative, unless and until the "just" society is created. Until then, speech as a means of peaceably *convincing* is in reality force, power, or manipulation disguised as speech. One of the common assumptions of this line of argument is that members of the unequal class have lost their autonomy: they can no longer reason or speak as free, independent minds; they have internalized the false ideas of the dominant class. Hence, speech is of no value to them unless and until enlightened elites who favor them "free up" the speech process.

In this chapter we evaluate and criticize the general argument that the demands of equality necessitate a restructuring of First Amendment doctrine. In the next chapter we concentrate on the contention that gender inequality requires censorship of pornography.

The new critics maintain that the victims of racist and sexist speech are weak and oppressed groups. They assert that blacks, gays, lesbians, and women do not occupy in substantial numbers positions of power in the media or the political structure. Free speech for these subjugated groups is a formality devoid of substance. The words that wound them not only cannot be effectively rebutted but also create stereotypes in society that reinforce the oppression and may create in the victims an acceptance of the stereotyping. Therefore, the alleged free market of ideas does not function for them. Perhaps worse, it is asserted, their autonomy and dignity—values advanced by free speech—are diminished by the false speech. Democratic values are cheapened by this process, since the oppression by hateful speech lessens their ability to participate on an equal basis in the democratic process. Hence, the role of free speech in advancing the processes of democracy—another value of free speech—is perverted by the words that wound.

The new critics argue that free speech in the classic liberal mode is obsolete. It was appropriate for an age and a society in which certain European whites were oppressed by more powerful groups of white males. It was an age in which great media giants had not yet arisen and individuals could more readily than today publish pamphlets and newspapers. Now that communications is in the hands of such giants, free speech is in reality speech for the owners and editors (mostly white males) of NBC, the *New York Times*, Time-Warner, or CBS. Individuals are submerged in such a society, divided from one another by self-interest. If individuals do have power, they are mostly of the Michael Milliken variety, wealthy and white, and, in the opinion of many, consumed by greed rather than inspired by communitarian impulses. The need, then, is for government to subsidize in some fashion the speech of genuine leaders of the African-American, Hispanic, gay, and lesbian communities, and that of women, and also to limit the speech of the wealthy and powerful. The new critics warn, by the way, that conservative prominent women and blacks are not genuinely female or black.

This is an old argument of orthodox Marxists, meta-morphosed into a philosophy of gender or race. They had theorized that the working classes were brainwashed by the dominant elites into a false consciousness that accepted the falsities of capitalism as truths. Free speech and debate were myths that could be transformed into reality only by the institution of a just society. Hence the communists, as leaders of the working classes, were the only genuine "speakers" for the oppressed. To the argument that the proletarian revolutionaries would become a new power elite, subjugating others, Marxist theory answered: "Marxist theory owed its freedom from ideological bias to the privileged possibilities of knowledge from a perspective of experience that had arisen with the position of the wage-laborer in the process of production. The argument was only cogent, however, within the framework of a philosophy of history that wanted to make the universal interest discernible in the class interest of the proletariat."[1]

The history of the twentieth century attests to the dangers of legitimating a monopoly on speech in the hands of the "leaders" of the proletariat at the expense of other classes. Efforts to support speech of certain groups and limit that of a despised hierarchy, because of the supposed fundamental, transcendental, and epistemological truth-frailty of such speech, are fraught with difficulty. As Jürgen Habermas puts it, "Those who conquer the theoretical avant-garde of today and overcome the current hierarchization of knowledge, themselves become the theoretical avant-garde of tomorrow and themselves establish a new hierarchy of knowledge. In any case, they cannot validate for their knowledge any superiority according to standards of truth claims that would transcend local agreements."[2]

This belittling of speech dehumanizes the groups to be

benefited. It is a method by which women or African-Americans who disagree with the prevailing orthodoxy of organized African-American or women's groups can be disregarded or belittled. It is a singularly elitist position, since it values the speech of "enlightened" leadership and deprecates that of members of the subjugated class who do not accept the views of the leadership.

All this is part of "unmasking theory" that, like Marx, points to a metadiscourse lying outside everyday speech that explains the true essence of things. Whether this universalistic explanation is class, gender, wealth, or race, it appeals to some deep structure in order to unlock the secrets of human society. As such, it acts as a reason to chill "false" discourse and advance the "truth." Truth is something out there, real and even transcendent, that has been discovered by philosophy—"our" philosophy, not yours.

That philosophy in the past was Marxism; now it is a philosophy of gender or race. It is a useful bludgeon with which to dismiss the opponent's argument as a "false" product of force rather than reason. It is a proposition that cannot be proved or disproved. The feminist who asserts that society is radically unjust and argues that, first, female speech (unless strengthened by governmental action) cannot be heard, and second, that female speech in opposition to her is a form of blithe and unwitting slavery, is confronted by religious fundamentalists who assert that portions of what she objects to are in the natural order of things.

The danger in using "inequality" as a method of equalizing speech (as opposed to equalizing acts or conduct, such as economic factors—although mandated economic equality has its own grave problems) is that it loosens our belief in the value of human dialogue. It maintains that the success or failure of speech is a roughly direct function of the wealth, status, or gender of the speaker. The Holmesian marketplace of ideas is abandoned. The role of speech in creating or preserving the autonomy of the speaker or listener is diminished. Finally, the role of speech as the essential core of the democratic process is questioned, because speech in the unjust society cannot facilitate the democratic process. Power, not human conversation, is elevated as the principal currency of the human condition.

The very choice of how to equalize speech carries with it explicit or implicit assumptions about truth and knowledge, and permissible and impermissible modes of persuasion. The assumption always is that the speech of certain powerful groups or individuals should be limited; the argument is that their speech is less than truthful. The choice of which "powerful" groups or individuals to limit is a matter of political agenda. Do we chill the power of powerful, liberal cinema moguls? Or of wealthy, liberal novelists? Do we equalize the power of a Reverend Jesse Jackson (liberal) and that of the conservative African-American Thomas Sowell? Indeed, what about genetic (assuming there are such, which I do not) or environmentally caused inequalities in individuals' persuasive powers? And what do we do when the worth and dignity of, for example, gay and lesbian groups gain predominance (as they should and probably will) and old, homophobic viewpoints are reduced to impotent minority status? Do we then equalize both sides, or do we decide that absolute truth has been reached in this important arena of discourse? In every society there will be groups and individuals with more power than other groups or individuals. How and where do we introduce the equalizing wedge? With wealth? In forms of business organization—for example, the publicly held corporation? With gender? With religion? Wealth plus religion? (Episcopalians have more power, due to inherited wealth, than do x religions: hence, chill their speech.) Do we do it with professional success? That is, do we chill the speech of successful professionals and subsidize that of the less effective? In all this, we are determining when speech "legitimately" persuades by some metaphysical notion of rationality and correspondence with truth out there, and not by some forbidden mode resulting from power.

"Power" is not a simple term. Speech at gunpoint is compelled; we can agree on that, but on little else. The speech of wealthy Nelson Rockefeller did not get him the Republican Party's nomination for president, whereas the speech of Ross Perot gave him a run for the presidency. Was the latter the result of illegitimate power or the complex result of persuasion? The analysis of that question, crudely put, will probably turn on who won or lost and whose social or political (agenda) ox was gored.

Arguments for limiting the ability of wealthy individuals to spend their money on their own campaigns are based upon powerful notions of the values of egalitarianism in political life. Money is power, and power is translatable into political clout, despite the failures of Perot and Rockefeller. The Supreme Court has rejected the aim of "equalizing the relative ability of individuals and groups to influence the outcome of elections."[3] The danger is the tendency of the inequality argument to create new elites, new centers of power that falsely assert some metaphysical proof of the justness of their newly found power. Allocation of speech power, in particular, when placed in the hands of government, creates enormous potential for bureaucratic control. At the present time, the federal government allocates millions of dollars to the major parties, whereby minority parties are placed at a great disadvantage. Do we subsidize them? Which groups? Skinheads? Libertarians? Religious fundamentalists? Egalitarianism in practice is never purely egalitarian. Some group or groups always control the government and decide who is to be equal and who is to be less than equal. As Justice Scalia recently stated, in a case limiting the ability of corporations to spend money on candidates in Michigan, the egalitarian argument permits the Court to limit any speaker, individual or corporate, whom or which it *believes* has "the mere *potential* for producing social harm."[4] Where do we draw the line? Do we strip the owners of the *New York Times* of their vast communication power? Does the government subsidize the political parties of designated subjugated groups?

The equalizing theory in speech turns out, with some mild deconstruction, to have a not-so-hidden agenda to create a revolutionary new society, egalitarian in wealth and power as defined by the government, and possessing certain attitudes toward gender, sexual preference, etc. What is uniquely dangerous in using speech limits to achieve the goal is that speech is the quintessential mode by which men and women understand, agree with, disagree with, withstand, or perceive the societal constraints, the status quo, and the need or lack of need for change. Chill it, delegitimate it, and we risk a return to authoritarian societies.

Ironically, "subjugated" speech cannot be rescued by individuals or associations that lack a critical mass of political clout. Fifty followers of a movement to revive the ancient religion of Zeus and the other Greek pagan gods will not get government subsidies for their speech. As Michael Novak has written, "In practice, allocative systems give superior benefits to those groups with superior organizational powers."[5] Egalitarian speech opportunities will probably be obtained by groups in American society that can move the levers of state and federal power. Necessarily, then, rival interest groups will agitate and lobby for government subsidies of their own speech and government chilling of the allegedly "quieting" speech of powerful groups. This will be done in the name of equality of speech, and in the spirit of increasing speech, but the actual results will be otherwise. Everyone will be equal, but, in Orwellian terms, more powerful groups will become more equal.

The new critics recommend using the judiciary and the legislature to channel free speech in order to achieve equality. Such speech as racist or sexist talk would be banned by statutory law or the common-law use of the tort of intentional emotional harm. Speech critical of non-subjugated groups would not be censored. The argument is that those groups do not need the protection of censorship, and so there is no reason to dilute First Amendment protection when weaker groups criticize them: "Harry is a honky" passes; "Bill is a nigger" is banned. However, allegedly racist and sexist speech extends well beyond the simple epithet. Limiting it to that category would permit a vast quantity of more subtle, more effective racist and sexist speech, at least as defined by many feminists and minority groups.

Therefore, courts will be tempted to extend the prohibited categories well beyond the simple three or four-letter epithet. Novels that disparage whites may be sold; novels that disparage blacks—in the opinion of some, *Huckleberry Finn* is an example—will be blocked. Novels or cinema scoffing at homosexuality will be banned; artistic work or nonfiction critical of the heterosexual nuclear family gets the green light. Roman Catholic teaching about the evils of homosexuality will be banned. Their teaching against birth control is suspect because its impact is arguably worse for poor minority families and women, who must bear the costs of large families. Speech recommending immigration laws that favor Europeans will be banned; that advocating immigration laws that favor Africans or Asians will be permitted. (Some minorities may argue that Asians succeed so well in America that they are no longer a subjugated group. That will have to be litigated.)

Speech criticizing quotas is presently on the borderline; the courts will have to determine whether such speech is inherently racist or sexist. Mainstream black groups consider quotas essential as one of the fundamental ways to end discrimination in our society—they may not consider it a borderline issue.

Speech criticizing busing is suspect; the courts will have to determine whether it subjugates the minority population. Speech attacking affirmative action programs will be suspect; again, the courts will have to determine whether it is protected by the First Amendment or is so injurious to minorities as to justify its censorship. Creative jurisprudence will be necessary concerning speech advocating the death penalty; such speech may, on judicial analysis, create a criminal justice structure that always executes blacks more frequently than whites.

So-called "classic" paintings depicting rape will be questionable, another issue to be considered by the courts. Likewise, great poems, such as *Leda and the Swan*, which describes a rape by Zeus, are questionable. Speeches, books, and articles emphasizing the role of women in the home may be censored. Beyond that, most literature more than fifty years old may be suspect, because of the degradation of women and minorities reflected in it. Speech advocating non-combat roles for women is at the margin; perhaps the courts will censor it—or perhaps not, since it argues sexual distinctions in the work force and hence is sexist. Scientific research that examines white deficiencies will be permitted; research that examines minority failings will be prohibited.

It is clear from this partial list that control of "racist and sexist" speech to accomplish equality involves monumental thought-control. That is not surprising, and it is what classic First Amendment liberalism has always predicted will flow from breaches of First Amendment content-neutrality. Unless we limit censorship to the simple epithet, such as "You are a kike," and budge not a whit from that simple category, the reach and scope of censorship will be enormous. But no meaningful doctrine that accepts the need to limit First Amendment protection in the interest of chilling sexist and racist speech can be successfully limited. Simple sexist and racial epithets, horrible as they are, are but the iceberg-tip of racial and sexist stereotyping, as the new critics see it. An

epithet is nothing but the crystallized street expression of racial and sexist bigotry. The reason for exempting it from First
Amendment protection is the falsity and perversity of the
thought.

Judicial doctrine will surely and inexorably reach out to
accomplish its purposes, and courts will soon be considering
the kinds of speech illustrated in the preceding paragraphs.
Since modern courts, as all attorneys and legal scholars know,
move creatively in constitutional law in search of what they
deem a proper mix of intent, policy, and morality, the boundaries of permissible speech will be governed by the justices'
visions of the evils of sexist and racist speech. Conservative
justices will reach one result, probably one not desired by the
new critics, and liberal, radical, or feminist justices will reach
another.

The movement toward a state-imposed vision of the good
society, if it materializes, would be the result of the abandonment of the traditional liberal version of the First Amendment. That philosophy was based upon an exaltation of the
individual and a healthy skepticism about the wisdom of the
state. Free speech facilitates the search for truth and permits
the self-realization of the individual. Tragically, that realiza-
tion does not always result in an admirable human being, but
it is a price we have to pay to avoid state authoritarianism and
thought-control by bureaucrats.

A distinguishing feature of humanity is its ability and capacity to entertain thought and opinion. Animals may have
some language, but humans are unique in the complexity and
subtlety of thinking. It is impossible, however, to separate
freedom of speech from freedom of inner thought. As Albert
Levi has said, "In a certain sense freedom of speech is as much
a concern of the inner life as is freedom of thought."[6] If we
limit it, as many post-liberal philosophers suggest, we move
inexorably toward a collectivist vision in which the state is
used to mold the ideal society as commanded by the then-

dominant forces in the culture. This is why, for example, fundamentalists and radical feminists have sometimes, albeit uneasily, joined forces to attempt to censor pornographic literature. Both groups, although wildly disparate, have strong notions of the right kind of society and also are disposed to use the state to advance them.

Note that I mentioned "dominant forces" above. The irony is that so-called subjugated groups can gain control over the direction of speech only by dominating the judiciary and the legislature. Their success marks the end of their subjugated status, unless we ascribe altruism to white dominant forces that grant them appropriate censorship. Professor Robert C. Post makes this point well:

> Paradoxically, therefore, the question of whether public discourse is inevitably damaged by racist speech must itself ultimately be addressed through the medium of public discourse. Because those participating in public discourse will not themselves have been silenced (almost by definition), a heavy, frustrating burden is de facto placed on those who would truncate public discourse in order to save it. They must represent themselves as "speaking for" those who have been deprived of their voice. But the negative space of that silence reigns inscrutable, neither confirming nor denying this claim. And the more eloquent the appeal, the less compelling the claim, for the more accessible public discourse will then appear to exactly the perspectives racist speech is said to repress.[7]

One of the barriers to the use of the state to create the ideal society, as seen by the politicians in command, is the First Amendment. Speech is a vital tool for molding attitudes. The state cannot effectively put its hand on that implement if individuals and private associations are free to speak out in opposition to state policy and if the state is limited in its use of power to coerce speech. The First Amendment operates as an obstacle to the politician's ability to create what he or she sees as a just society.

The new critics emphasize the need for equality. They argue that the Fourteenth Amendment's equal-protection clause emphasizes the value of equality in society.[8] Subjugated groups, arguably, lack the power necessary for competition in the market for ideas; hence, racist speech no matter how broadly construed, must be censored. Other nasty speech, it has been suggested, such as flag burning, may be protected, since the victims include offended powerful, patriotic, establishment conservatives.

The argument from equality is designed to censor speech that dissents from the prevailing politically correct vision of the just society. This is a position that endorses a particular political orthodoxy as a systemic limit on free speech. As such it runs counter to the philosophical core of free speech and the First Amendment.[9] As the Court stated in *United States v. J. Eichman*, the case which voided the Flag Protection Act of 1989, "We are aware that desecration of the flag is deeply offensive to many, but the same might be said, for example, of virulent ethnic and religious epithets, vulgar repudiations of the draft, and scurrilous caricatures. If there is a bedrock principle underlying the First Amendment, it is that the Government may not prohibit the expression of an idea simply because society finds the idea itself offensive or disagreeable."[10]

More particularly, banning speech offensive to the less powerful would in reality chill speech that disagrees with the prevailing "educated" view of who or what is a subjugated class deprived of free speech. For example, are gays a subjugated group requiring speech priority? Those who disagree, such as the leadership of the Roman Catholic Church, may find that their free speech is chilled because of a politically correct determination of values regarding subjugation. (Are Roman Catholic bishops a subjugated minority?)

This question as to the proper identity of the subjugated may go to the heart of the current argument from equality. Conservatives bitterly argue, perhaps to the point of boredom, that the elite media is controlled by liberals. There is persuasive polling data that confirms their dim view. Recent studies demonstrate that almost 90 percent of journalists voted for Clinton and consider themselves liberal politically. Hence, conservatives complain, there is a systemic inequality in control of the media (and, they always add, of elite universities, whose faculties share the same liberal bias).

Evangelical fundamentalists argue that they are despised by the educated media elites.[11] As Richard Neuhaus puts it, "For most Americans blessed or blighted by higher education, everything associated with fundamentalism has been indelibly poisoned. . . . Fundamentalism . . . represents all the bigotry, know-nothingness, and legalistic repression that has ever afflicted humankind."[12] Fundamentalists were, until recent years, excluded from the "public square," that is, the political life of the country.[13] In recent years they have made a foray into that area by influencing the Republican Party.[14] Certainly, in their opinion, they are a frustrated and oppressed minority; do we then structure government control of speech to compensate them for their lack of equality in the world of ideas and opinion formation? They might suggest the following measures: quota hiring of fundamentalists in elite universities; quota offerings on fundamentalism in universities; quota publication of fundamentalist ideas in elite journals; quota hiring of fundamentalist reporters for elite newspapers; quota hiring of creationist scientists in elite universities; production of one pro-fundamentalist movie for every three anti-fundamentalist movies; or right of reply in the editorial page for every anti-fundamentalist editorial. Naturally, such epithets as "*X* is an Elmer Gantry" will be banned. To the extent that speech molds behavior, such measures would indeed create a different America.

In short, the very choice of the disadvantaged groups is a matter of vigorously debated opinion and fact. Who deserves more speech protection, Hispanics, Blacks, or Asians? Do Mexicans or Puerto Ricans more than other Hispanics? Koreans more or less than other Asians? The example of fundamentalists illustrates that introducing speech control in the interest of disadvantaged groups will amount to massive government control as to which groups dominate speech, which groups must get more free speech, and in general, as to sovereignty over the spiritual, moral, religious, ethnic, and political direction of society. It will constitute a move in the direction of an authoritarian state, or even of a totalitarian state. It is a move toward rigid quotas in the arena of speech. The losers in the free market will always argue that they are subjugated. They will always, if we permit breach of the First Amendment, seek out government thought-control to redress the balance and shift it in their direction.

In this regard, there is some wisdom to be gained from a recent incident in Hawaii that illustrates the complexities we invite when we begin to pit group against group and attempt to determine which has privileged speech because of subjugation. A white student at the University of Hawaii complained in a student newspaper about "Caucasian bashing," claiming that "racism is not an exclusively white endeavor." A faculty member wrote a letter to the newspaper attacking white prejudice against ethnic Hawaiians and asking him to leave the state. She maintained that the student "did not understand racism at all." He did fly home, but he intended to return the following semester. Some critics called the faculty member a racist, and the faculty of the philosophy department, in which the student had been enrolled, criticized the faculty member who had written the letter. Her supporters argued for her right to free speech. The University Center for Hawaiian Studies characterized the philosophy department as involved in "plantation tactics of threat." The argument involved use of the word "*haole*," a Hawaiian word that once meant foreigner but now means a Caucasian. The student had claimed that native Hawaiians use the word in a derogatory sense. Caucasians constitute 24 percent of Hawaii's population; Japanese-Americans constitute 23 percent; ethnic and part-Hawaiians make up 20 percent; and Filipinos constitute 11 percent, but are the most rapidly increasing group. Caucasians and Asian-Americans are the economically most successful groups.[15]

An important article by Mari J. Matsuda also illustrates the dangers and difficulties of affording more speech protection to "disadvantaged" groups and less to more powerful ones. She makes the specific suggestion that hateful speech by disadvantaged groups should be protected by the First Amendment;[16] vicious anti-white epithets by minorities should be protected. Whites directing the same kind of speech against blacks, let us say, would be subjected to criminal prosecution. She then examines, as she puts it, "stories at the edge."[17] These are "problem"[18] cases under her definition of actionable racist speech. A problem for her is Zionism and Zionist speech.[19] Is it racist speech? If it is, are Jews a disadvantaged group? She reassures us by asserting, "I reject the sweeping charge that Zionism is racism and argue instead for a highly contextualized consideration of Zionist speech."[20] Zionists, she believes, are "off the hook," but not always; it depends on the context.[21] I trust the reader gets the message: once we enter the domain of emasculating the First Amendment in order to censor all varieties of allegedly racist speech, we get into such highly political arguments as, Is Zionism racism?

Professor Matsuda then asserts that "[t]o the extent any racial hostility expressed within a Zionist context is a reaction to historical prosecution, it is protected under the doctrinal scheme suggested [of protecting racist speech of prosecuted groups] in this article."[22] This means that courts will examine whether Zionists critique Arab tactics and policies, and whether the level of critique reaches what the court determines to be "racist." Then courts will decide whether Jews are technically a disadvantaged group. No doubt, one side will call Arab experts and the other will call Jewish experts on this issue.

Professor Matsuda then argues that if the Zionist asserts "generic white supremacy,"[23] this constitutes Jewish alliance with the dominant group, and the Jewish speaker loses his or her privilege to criticize Arabs harshly. (Perhaps if the Jewish speaker is a woman, she will be able to trump the litigation against her on the grounds that she is part of a subjugated sex.)

Matsuda's next difficult issue is whether blacks and other minorities may engage in anti-Semitic speech.[24] This question presents a knotty issue for her, since here one subordinated group is castigating another. She analyzes the problem in one sentence: "I am inclined to prohibit such speech."[25] However, she would sometimes rely on the culture of the recipient group. She argues that "the custom in a particular subordinated community may tolerate racial insults as a form of word play."[26] She would judge it by the recipient's "community standard."[27]

There is no doubt that under her scheme the state or the private plaintiff will be free to attempt to prove that Jews are not subordinated. This attempt may involve such issues of proof as wealth of Jews, what industries they allegedly dominate, their SAT scores, and the size of their average home. The weakness in her argument is inherent in the approach whereby freedom of speech turns on the relative dominance or subordination of a group. It is a subject that calls for political, social, and emotional arguments of the most extreme subjectivity and personal bias. There will always be real and alleged power imbalances. In the United States, white Anglo-Saxon Protestants, Japanese, Chinese, and Jews enjoy higher economic status than Mexicans, Blacks, Native Americans, and Puerto Ricans.[28] But certain groups are more successful politically while less successful economically. The Japanese were "relatively late participants in politics on the mainland."[29] For many years, the Irish enjoyed more political than economic power.[30] Powerful families own the *New York Times* and the *Washington Post*. Males dominate the hierarchy of the Roman Catholic Church.

The speech-equality philosophy of the new critics cannot be contained. It requires a powerful state organ to command speech equality, as they define it, across society. The kind of society that can expropriate control of the *New York Times* and *Washington Post* from inherited wealth, censor allegedly anti-feminist propaganda of the Catholic hierarchy, and chill the speech of more successful ethnic groups, is the kind of society that was predominant in Eastern Europe until a few years ago, when it collapsed. It is a totalitarian society that requires a governing elite that must appropriate all power, including power over speech, for itself and the groups it decides to favor.

We have emphasized the nature of the liberal society as characterized by debate and persuasion. There is obviously a difference between free debate and force. But we move into tricky cases when we attempt to decide which speech is free and which is the product of so-called hierarchical structures, what the Marxists call "false consciousness."

In our society there is seldom a political consensus as to what opinions are the result of "good" or "rational" persuasion, in contrast to dominant group trickery or deceit (i.e., "force"). Indeed, that is inherently a peculiarly difficult and dangerous distinction, often made for partisan advantage. For example, some business groups argue that corporate executives and business people in general are uniformly excoriated by left-wing media elites in television programs and sitcoms, resulting in a kind of anti-business brainwashing. Traditionalists—that is Catholic and Protestant fundamentalists—insist, as mentioned above, that speech is unfairly distributed among the so-called cultural elites. That was the political battle cry of Vice President Dan Quayle in the 1992 election campaign. Many feminists argue that sexist and pornographic speech in the workplace and elsewhere is a product of deep cultural inequities imposed by right-wing reactionaries. The courts and the federal legislature (see Title VII and the discussion in the next chapter) are convinced that speech in the workplace involves issues of "force," not "persuasion." But both working-class and white-collar males who relish pornographic speech will no doubt argue that the speech is a voluntary choice that does not reflect unacceptable inequalities. The very legitimacy or illegitimacy of many inequalities is at issue. What certain feminists view as inequality is viewed by some traditionalists as the natural order of things. Traditionalists contend that the male-female relationships in existence for centuries do not reveal inequality but instead represent a fundamental fairness resulting from essential differences between men and women. However, traditionalists and certain feminists reach accord on issues of pornographic speech.

As we move in society into radical new patterns of thought, old groups will view virtually all of the language of new groups as entirely irrational, and vice versa. Each group will view all the thoughts of the other as the result of emotion, deceit, force, and trickery. The arguments of each group will be considered a matter to be turned over to the censors. This is what happens today in disputes between religious fundamentalists, gays and lesbians, feminists, secular humanists, the bishops of the Catholic Church, and minority groups in our troubled society.

NOTES

1. Jürgen Habermas, *The Philosophical Discourse of Modernity* 280–1 (Frederick G. Laurence, trans., 1987).

2. *Id.* at 281.

3. Buckley v. Valeo, 424 U.S. 1, 48 (1976).

4. Austin v. Michigan Chamber of Commerce, 494 U.S. 652, 689 (1990) (Scalia, J., dissenting).

5. Michael Novak, *The Spirit of Democratic Capitalism* 124 (1982).

6. Albert Levi, in John Stuart Mill, *On Liberty* (D. Spitz, ed., 1975) at 196.

7. Robert C. Post, *Racist Speech, Democracy, and the First Amendment in* Speaking of Race, Speaking of Sex 146 (1994).

8. *See e.g.*, Mari J. Matsuda, *Public Response to Racist Speech: Considering the Victim's Story* 87 Mich. L. Rev. 2320 (1989).

9. Some have argued that *Brown v. Board of Education*, 347 U.S. 483 (1954), justifies censorship of private racist speech. That case, it is said, established a principle of racial equality that encompasses speech. However, *Brown* forbade *state* racist *conduct*, not *private speech*. To conflate speech with conduct, and governmental action with private speech, is a fundamental error. Even if *Brown* implicitly forbade government racist speech, it cannot forbid private racist speech. Nadine Strossen, *Regulating Racist Speech on Campus: A Modest Proposal*, 1990 Duke L.J. 484, 542–7.

10. United States v. Eichman, 110 S. Ct. 2404, 2409–10 (1990) (cite omitted).

11. Richard J. Neuhaus, *The Naked Public Square: Religion and Democracy in America* (1984).

12. *Id.* at 45.

13. *Id.* at ch. 3.

14. *Id.* at 35.

15. Richard Halloran, *Hawaii Journal: Rare Storm over Race Ruffles a Mixed Society*, N.Y. Times, Dec. 26, 1990, at A20.

16. Matsuda, *supra* note 8, at 2361–4.

17. *Id.* at 2361.

18. *Id.*

19. *Id.* at 2364.
20. *Id.*
21. *Id.*
22. Matsuda, *supra* note 8, at 2364.
23. *Id.*
24. *Id.* at 2363–4.
25. *Id.* at 2364.
26. *Id.* (cite omitted).
27. *Id.*
28. Thomas Sowell, *Ethnic America* 5 (1981).
29. *Id.* at 179.
30. *Id.* at 30–9.

CHAPTER 5

EROTICISM, OBSCENITY, PORNOGRAPHY, AND FREE SPEECH

Modern society speaks about sex, Michel Foucault observes, "*ad infinitum*, while exploiting it as *the* secret."[1] As he pointed out, we attempt to explain virtually everything about ourselves in terms of sex. We "bring [ourselves] almost entirely—our bodies, our minds, our individuality, our history—under the sway of a logic of concupiscence and desire."[2]

Sexual depiction, in the forms modern society terms "pornography" or "obscenity," is a multibillion-dollar industry.[3] It is also the object of regulatory concern by the government and important movements in society.[4] The debate about pornography begins with one fundamental question: What is it?[5] The hotly disputed answers inevitably turn on (sometimes violently) contrasting notions of the good and evil life.[6] Pornography is a running debate about issues deep in the human psyche, issues more fundamental than virtually any other of the political topics that constitute core First Amendment debates.[7]

Many religious conservatives and also many feminists believe they can both define and justifiably condemn pornography. Their reasons often differ, but they agree that pornography lacks intellectual or aesthetic merit, or inflicts hurt to a level that demands abrogation of First Amendment protection for pornographic speech. Their ideological opponents argue that what some would decry as harmful "porn" is occasionally great art, or at least may be a positive contribution to sexual freedom and liberation.[8]

In American constitutional law, pornography, whatever it is, is not identical to obscenity. Obscenity is a legal term; it is the depiction of sexual conduct that appeals to the prurient interest, is patently offensive, and lacks serious value.[9] Crudely put, it is repulsive sex that lacks value. The harm in obscenity is the damage it does to the traditional, ordered moral fabric of society.[10] What is moral or repulsive and what is of value are notoriously subjective and murky concepts. Obscene speech is not protected by the First Amendment.

Pornography, if it is anything, refers in some sense to the depiction of sexual organs or conduct.[11] The word "pornography" proliferated and gained fame when erotica, which had previously appeared only in the libraries of the upper classes, began to be merchandised to the masses after the French Revolution. The response was official governmental censorship.[12]

Pornography includes material that may have serious value. Accordingly, the definition of pornography is broader than that of obscenity. Although adult pornography is not definitively excluded from First Amendment protection,[13] the Supreme Court has decided that near-obscene speech is less equal than other categories of speech.[14] Further, those who display pornography in the workplace may be subject to civil prosecution under Title VII of the Civil Rights Act.[15]

This chapter examines the meanings of pornography, eroticism, and obscenity. These terms are complex, vague, and controversial. They merge into each other and reflect the differing and wildly controversial attitudes of different cultures and times. In the course of discussing these issues this chapter attempts to demonstrate that the terms pornography, eroticism, and obscenity involve a *dispute* about some of the deepest issues in the human condition. This dispute affects any consideration of the relationship between the First Amendment and words or pictures that are erotic or pornographic. This chapter suggests that, ironically, the reason courts do not protect the obscene (as defined by the Supreme Court) and give only grudging protection to the near-obscene is that these words and pictures involve concerns that are *immeasurably more important* than the mundane political issues that are customarily given full First Amendment protection. Indeed, many distinguished thinkers suggest that pornography should lose its current First Amendment protection because of the overwhelming evil significance, as they see it, of the issues presented by the use of pornography. The result of this type of pressure is ever-increasing censorship.

The first section begins with a brief review of the cultural and religious attitudes toward sex and sexual behavior in the West. It briefly sketches the contrasting attitudes of the ancient Greeks, Christianity, and Judaism and then mentions some modern variations on the theme. This backdrop is designed to emphasize that the sexual behavior that society condemns (and therefore the art that depicts it) is a product of deep and conflicting cultural and religious constructs. Thus, an ancient Greek vase with erotic nude paintings that depict sodomy and masturbation might be considered pornographic today by certain religious groups, but clearly it was celebrated and approved in that culture.[16]

The next section discusses the rise of the modern concept of pornography as an object of official regulation in the West, which reached an apogee at the time of the French Revolution. During this period pornography was a political weapon in the hands of opponents of repressive autocratic regimes. The politicization of this subject continues today. Modern pornography is essentially art or hack-work (erotica) that is disapproved of by influential and powerful interests. When pornography is banned, it is an indication that these interests have won the debate by ending it.

The third section analyzes the formidable contemporary feminist argument that pornography is a male weapon used for the establishment and maintenance of a paternalistic society. The fourth, concluding, section suggests that regulation of pornography (and obscenity) is a result of society's desire to choke off those viewpoints that it finds deeply and dangerously offensive—indeed, far more offensive than the usual political debate that the First Amendment traditionally protects. Pornography and obscenity are debates about issues so important that courts are disposed to limit the argument and limit free speech.

CULTURAL AND RELIGIOUS ATTITUDES TOWARD SEX

At the very outset, the term "pornographic" is problematic. Is a classic Greek nude statue pornographic? Are *National Geographic* videos showing copulating animals pornographic? Are *Romeo and Juliet* (with its explicit sexual jokes) or *The Taming of the Shrew* (with its depiction of a male dominating his future wife) to be considered pornography? Is the film industry, which continually depicts men and women in varying stages of undress or in simulated sexual acts, pornographic? Is the biblical story of the seduction of Lot by his daughters pornographic? If pornography is simply the more or less graphic depiction of sex or sexual organs, we have an impossibly broad category.[17]

Inevitably, society imposes normative constructs as it attempts to define pornography. Indeed, pornography is not a "thing" but an "argument" between institutions of the state and artists, good and bad, as to what is permissible in the realm of depiction of sexual behavior.[18] As the Meese Commission observed, pornography " 'seems to mean in practice any discussion or depiction of sex to which the person using the word objects.' "[19] Almost any frank depiction or even discussion of sex is likely to enrage some segment of society. Pornography is a concept that cannot be defined without taking a particular ideological, religious, or moral position on fundamental views of life. Any attempted definition of pornography contains a philosophical viewpoint of what constitutes an ethically acceptable society.

For example, in 1993 a Western reporter described the Iranian mobilization against "pop music and other horrors."[20] The article reported as immoral those who listened to Western pop music and women who wore lipstick or exposed strands of their hair.[21] In the opinion of Iranian religious leaders, such conduct, and its depiction, will lead to prostitution and atheism. What is considered acceptable and, indeed, commendable in Western society is condemned in another society as pornographic. Although cultural relativism is no great surprise, sometimes its enormity is impressive.

The social dynamite inherent in the definition of pornography results from the picturing or description of sex. Inescapably, sex and desire are the subject and object of powerful religious and cultural forces. As Camille Paglia said, "Eros, like Dionysus, is a great and dangerous God."[22] Society either permits or circumscribes sex and depictions of sex depending on the religious and political assertions of the harm (or lack of it) of certain practices.[23] It follows that different cultures will disagree as to what depicts sex (lipstick?), what is explicit sex (exposed strands of women's hair?), and the like. Put crudely, pornography is in the eye of the beholder.

The dispute over the definition of pornography involves the deepest views possible about the nature of the good (or evil) of society. Differences as to tax policy, free trade, and the like pale before the stakes involved in the definition of pornography. Inevitably, when a court or other organ of the state labels a painting, book, or film as pornographic, it has made a fundamental, viewpoint-based judgment about speech.

Since the First Amendment is designed, at the very minimum, to protect against viewpoint censorship, it is peculiar that obscenity is denied First Amendment protection and that near-obscenity frequently gets only diluted protection.[24] Perhaps sex is actually far more important than political speech and hence, in the opinion of the Court, cannot be left safely to a free market of speech.

In modern Western society, the contours of permitted sexual practice are changing as notions of harmful sex are altered. In Iran, because of the supposedly dangerous seductiveness of women but not men, women are allowed to appear in public only if swathed in black cloth. In the United States, however, women are more or less free to dress as they please. A few decades ago, sex in American films was limited to a chaste embrace; today, sex is explicit. America seems awash with sex (and violence) in theaters, movies, novels, television, and in commercials for everything from automobiles to soap. Fifty years ago there were established, "traditional" codes of behavior between women and men:[25] sex outside the marriage bond was immoral;[26] divorce was abnormal;[27] sexual passion on the part of women was regarded with alarm, if not horror; and homosexuality was "in the closet" and judged to be deviant, immoral, and criminal.[28]

Today, due to the sexual revolution and the changing roles and status of women, gays, and lesbians, the codes have changed radically and are in constant flux. The very definitions of sexuality for men and women are constantly being redefined. The value and definition of concepts of family, love, marriage, and romance have become the subject of rancorous debate and controversy. For example, more children are now born out of wedlock.[29] Gay and lesbian lifestyles are celebrated in the dominant culture of theater and art. Perhaps most significantly, feminists have directed our attention to the social, political, and sexual subordination of women as a construct of relations between women and men.[30] Many feminists persuasively argue that rape, including date rape and marital rape, is endemic in our society.[31] They assert that frequently what passes for sex is violence by men against women.[32] Some women view heterosexual intercourse in many contexts of male domination as a form of violent dominion of men over women.[33]

Religious conservatives are traditionalists in sexual matters. (They do not, however, want to go back to the love of boys in fourth-century B.C. Greece.) They take their religious scriptures seriously and literally. The nuclear family—mother, father, children—is central to the good life.[34] (In response, some political liberals are beginning to take the point, if not the lead, on this argument about the need for the family.[35]) In their belief, marriage is more than a private relationship; it is the essential moral cement that binds together a healthy society. Sex is moral only in the marriage relationship. Lust is forbidden, since it tends to breach the marriage bonds. They assert that gay and lesbian sex is immoral and unnatural. Even heterosexual sex is suspect when divorced from the procreative purpose.

In the Catholic Church, sex itself is suspect, even when related to marriage; hence, the clergy are celibate in order to follow higher pursuits. The Christian aversion to sex is well pictured in the following statements. St. Augustine emphasized that we are *"inter faeces et urinam nascimur"* ("born between feces and urine").[36] Nietzsche stated, "Christianity gave Eros poison to drink. He did not die, but became vice."[37] Georges Bataille stated that "Christianity associated eroticism unambiguously with evil. What in paganism was only the momentary reversal of the course of things became the lot of the damned, the share that came under God's eternal curse."[38]

For religious conservatives, even nudity is suspect; certainly they would argue that public displays of nudity are immoral (perhaps even private displays). Georges Bataille pointed out

that not so long ago Christian religious institutions required
girls to enter bathtubs in long nightgowns.[39] As Allan Bloom
wrote, discussing the historical differences between the Judeo-Christian tradition and the ancient Greeks on sexuality:

> The Greeks' naked exercises, including those at the
> Olympic games, scandalized the Jews . . . but they also
> attracted many of their young. . . . But the gymnasia
> were not all that was objectionable about the Greeks.
> They were regarded as secondary emanations from their
> principal cause, Greek philosophy, which was quickly
> identified with Epicureanism, interpreted as the unbri-
> dled pursuit of pleasure. Among serious Jews, the very
> name Epicurus, in a Hebrew or Yiddish form, is still an
> ugly epithet.[40]

Religious conservatives believe that Eros is a powerful and
dangerous (perhaps evil) force that must be severely disci-
plined and channeled into a sharply defined, acceptable path,
the nuclear family.[41] In Orthodox Judaism, the family is central; Eros is bound up in the husband-wife relationship. As an
Orthodox rabbi recently wrote, "Judaism prohibits adultery,
premarital sex, pederasty, bestiality and other activities that at
least some subset of the population desires. . . . Compulsive
sexuality—homosexual or heterosexual—is a mental disorder.
. . . *Kiddushin*, the sanctity of marriage and of sexuality in
marriage, is fundamentally violated by compulsive sexuality of
any type."[42] He further stated, "The family is our most important religious institution; a homosexual partnership is not
a family."[43]

The family was made primary in orthodox Judaism, and
sexuality outside of wedlock was condemned. A conservative
Jewish writer asserted, "Judaism may be said to have invented
the notion of homosexuality, for in the ancient world sexuality was not divided between heterosexuality and homosexuality. . . . Jews placed controls on sexual activity. It was to

be sanctified . . . and placed in the . . . bed of husband and wife."[44] The great Moses Maimonides wrote that circumcision was designed "to limit sexual intercourse."[45] It "counteracts excessive lust" but does not "destroy the power of generation."[46] As he further explained, professional harlots were not tolerated in ancient Israel, because they would tend to weaken family bonds.[47]

The family is considered essential in Judaism because family members are united by love; they exist to help each other and to lessen the strife that inevitably accompanies the breakdown of the family. Maimonides stated that "we ought to limit sexual intercourse altogether, hold it in contempt, and desire it only rarely."[48] Homosexuality is forbidden since, "[i]f in the natural way the act is too base to be performed except when needed, how much more base is it if performed in an unnatural manner, and only for the sake of pleasure."[49] Maimonides tempered this, however, by saying that "we must keep in everything the golden mean; we must not be excessive in love, but must not suppress it entirely; for the Law commands, 'be fruitful, and multiply.' "[50] He pointed out that circumcision leaves the "natural faculty in full force, but is guarded against excess."[51]

If I may generalize, the Jews never endorsed asceticism, as did Christians; however, they fell far short of Greek and Roman sexual liberality.[52] Despite some of the implications of Maimonides's statements, the Jews did not disapprove of sexual pleasure and, unlike the Catholic Church, they rejected celibacy.[53] Western Jews permitted polygamy up until the eleventh century, and Eastern Jews until the twentieth century.[54] Modern liberal Jews do not share Maimonides's sexology, and many non-Orthodox rabbis either welcome practicing homosexuals into Judaism or at least are currently reconsidering the meaning of the ancient taboos.[55]

Modern conservatives who emphasize the value of sex in marriage do not rely solely on theological grounds; rather, they assert that women domesticate the wild nature of men in the marriage bond.[56] Thus, bachelors are far more likely than married men to live for the short term and neglect the "long horizons" of career and stability.[57] Ironically, some modern liberals have begun to adopt this argument in the face of the endemic violence in American culture.[58]

In contrast, the classical Greeks did not view sex as inherently problematical.[59] Yet the Greeks did not view sex as neutral or as always benign.[60] The concept of moderation[61] and the distinction between the active and the passive were central to the Greek view of sex.[62] The virtuous man—and Greek books were written exclusively for men by men[63]—modulated his quantity of sex. This was important as a method by which the good man created a proper balance in his life and a proper control over self. The man who learned to control himself was then, and only then, capable of exercising leadership over free citizens of the city-state.[64] Michel Foucault, in his description of the ancient Greeks, quoted Aristotle as saying that "self-indulgent individuals exceed . . . in all these ways; they both delight in some things that they ought not to delight in, and if one ought to delight in some of the things they delight in, they do so more than one ought and than most men do."[65]

The act of penetration was also central to the concept of activity and passivity in sex for Greek men.[66] The virtuous man was one who was active, not passive, in his sexual contacts, whether with boys or with women. The gender of his partner did not matter (with certain qualifications discussed below), so long as the man was the penetrator.[67] This active man also merited dominance in the world of politics.[68] If Foucault's history is correct, the classical Greek mix of sex and politics confirms feminist arguments about the systemic domination of women by men. The Greeks asserted that women were naturally subordinate and, hence, naturally passive, i.e., penetratees.[69] For this reason, the Greeks condemned lesbianism; it required, they believed, one of the female partners to take an active or masculine role, and that was considered unnatural.[70] Similarly, the Greeks approved of the missionary position, because it expressed male superiority.[71] (They apparently regarded the proper role of the worthy man as on top, whether with boy, man, or woman.)

The relationship between boy and man was applauded in ancient Greece. But the relationship had its inherent difficulties. Unlike the wife, the free-born boy would as an adult become a leader in the family and the city-state. Hence, his relationship with his lover was one of more or less equals—unlike that of husband and wife—and was itself tricky.[72] As a beloved, the boy ran the risk, if the relationship were consummated, of being the penetratee. Since this would place him in an ignoble position, the Greek philosophers and poets created intricate mating rituals to disguise his position.[73]

The young Greek boy who openly expressed desire was suspect. He was to consent to the act only in the guise of offering a sort of assistance to the ardor of the adult lover. The adult lover who desired consummation was desiring an act that put into question the future leadership role of the boy. Therefore, the better relationship involved an idealistic, non-sexual adult lover, who sought to educate his beloved rather than place his hand beneath the boy's tunic. For instance, Socrates, the lover of the Good, was lauded for his asceticism and his denial of the carnal inducements of the great Alcibiades.[74] Hence, the ideal man-boy relationship was one that facilitated the search for the true and the beautiful.[75] What in practice occurred in these relationships we do not know with certainty, since we have theories and myths but no empirical data.[76]

Homosexuality as we know it today, although suspect, was not the subject of great interest or moral concern.[77] Since it was ignoble to take the passive role in the sex act, the adult male relationship was troubling.[78] (The Greeks apparently could not easily conceive of relationships of sexual equality between adult males.) There was no concept among the Greeks that paralleled our modern bipolarity of sexuality—that is, our distinction between heterosexuality and homosexuality.[79] As mentioned, the Greeks distinguished between the penetrator and the penetratee; sameness of gender was not an issue.

In the fourth century before the Common Era, the Greeks extolled the relationship between man and boy, but the conjugal relationship was expressed in severely male-dominant terms. The wife (often in her teens when married) was controlled by the husband.[80] Sex between them was a method of creating heirs for the elites, and marriage was a method of preserving and passing on property.[81] (We cannot say about the poor, who did not write about themselves.) Needless to say, the husband was free to take male or female lovers, and slaves of either sex were always fair game. The wife was expected to be faithful; her principal "right" was to be free from the presence of a rival woman in the home.[82]

During a gradual evolution of the marriage concept in the first centuries of the Common Era,[83] philosophers began to argue that the relationship between husband and wife was more important and more satisfactory than that of man to boy.[84] Elite opinion began to emphasize reciprocal relationships and notions of equality (including fidelity) in the marriage relationship.[85] The dangers of sex received greater emphasis, yet never reached the Christian notions of inherent evil.[86] The man-boy love relationship, however, continued to be accepted and to be lauded in elite opinion, and the man continued to dominate the marriage relationship.

This discussion of Greek and Roman sexuality relies on Foucault's famous histories of sexuality. The relevance of sexual power relationships is characteristic of Foucault's general methods and ideology in other fields. His works are characterized by the argument that beneath the appearance of reason or biology exists the reality of power relationships shaping all societal forms. Camille Paglia will have none of that.[87] She points out that many Greek and Roman men "found both women and boys desirable but that boys' sexual attractiveness ended when they sprouted a beard and body hair."[88] She asserts that "there is an aesthetic issue here, vividly documented from Archaic monody through Roman satire, in praise of the girlish rosiness, smoothness, and glow of boys' flesh."[89] But Foucault speaks of sex only in the language of power and subordination; sexuality is reduced to the "ethos of penetration and domination."[90] Paglia describes this as a "display of old-maidish puritanism," a "scholarship reduced to *Mad* magazine parody."[91] As she sarcastically summarizes it, "All those Greeks banging away had no idea they were having sex without sexuality. They were merely discoursing on power, you see."[92] Paglia mocked Foucault's notion that women and boys were merely passive objects—"just sperm spittoons."[93] She derides Foucault's implication that women then (or now) are always victims: "His attempt to make the body the passive property of male society is an evasion of the universal fact so intolerable to him: that we are all born of human mothers. By turning women into ciphers of men, he miniaturizes and contains them."[94] As she elegantly states, "Foucault sees power everywhere except where it is greatest: the female principle."[95]

Paglia's criticism of Foucault[96] is remarkably similar to that of the distinguished European philosopher, Jürgen Habermas, who faulted Foucault for ignoring the complexities and nuances of human relationships, including sexuality. As he puts it, Foucault has leveled "ambiguous phenomena,"[97] ignoring the magic, mystery, and biology (as well as culture) inherent in sexuality. Similarly, another European philosopher, Jean-François Revel, recounted how Foucault, in a conference devoted to analyzing Soviet dictatorship, argued that the conferees were ignoring the Gulag that was the West. Russian representatives to the meeting, who had had experience with the real Gulag, could not contain their amazement at his reductionism of everything in the West to brute, coercive power.[98]

Whatever one may think of Paglia's critique, it is obvious that, unlike with the ancient Greeks and Romans, the man-boy erotic relationship is especially problematical in modern Western society. This relationship has even been criminalized. Few today would write, as did Aristophanes in his play *The Birds*, of a dissident longing for freedom from the oppressive city and its laws to practice pederasty.[99]

Bloom argued that the "Bible teaches us an intense but severely limited eroticism,"[100] one limited to the nuclear family. Perhaps Bloom wrongly described this eroticism as "intense." For the Greeks, "the erotic ties were more diffuse and . . . concentrated less on fidelity than on the quest for the beautiful, wherever it may be found."[101] (Of course, the philosophers also may have been justifying their occasional reach under the boy's tunic.) This does not mean, necessarily, that the Greeks emphasized (at least in theory) the carnal. On the contrary, Alcibiades complained that try as he might to seduce Socrates, he failed. Plato viewed Eros as an education in the pursuit of the Good.[102]

In contrast to Foucault's emphasis on sex as an empirical example of power, Georges Bataille defined eroticism as a temporary return to nature, involving a "dialectic of prohibition and transgression."[103] Men and women became distinguished as human when they turned away from nature. Animals have no repugnance for excrement, filth, or sex in whatever form, place, or time. Although men and women became human when they erected sacred taboos and prohibitions, in the pagan world a momentary return to unlimited sex, including the orgy, was permitted as a temporary "reversal of the course of things."[104] "Sensuous excess"[105] provided "access to the sacred"[106] in some mysterious fashion. In response, Christianity and Judaism viewed the prohibitions as absolute. Christianity totally divided Eros (evil) from the religious. While the pagan world linked the religious and the sexual, "Christianity associated eroticism unambiguously with evil."[107] Bataille asserted: "In fact, these elements [taboos and prohibitions] were an inducement, and we have seen that eroticism owes its value to the distaste we have for the animality of sex."[108] He emphasizes that the "horror" of taboo transgression plays an essential role in Eros.[109] Eros is attractive because it "uses up our strength and our resources and, if necessary, places our life in danger."[110]

Bataille argues that norms are binding because we believe them to be sacred, and they are enticing because of the experiences of sacrilege felt when we violate them.[111] He believes that modern religion is responsible for having severed the link between the sacred and the profane. Bataille further asserts that modern, industrialized, capitalistic life has lead to a vitiation of the sacred, an emasculation of eroticism, and a kind of attenuation of the sense of divine terror and anxiety that was closely allied to primitive religion. If eroticism properly reemerges, it could create a new exuberance and vitality that would lead to a form of economics based upon plenty rather than scarcity, on life-enhancing activity rather than war.[112]

THE RISE OF MODERN CONCEPTS OF PORNOGRAPHY

Many societies have produced portrayals of various forms of eroticism, including the explicit depiction of sexual organs and acts. But the modern notion of pornography as a distinct regulatory category seems to have arisen subsequent to the 1500s and to have been solidified in the eighteenth and nineteenth centuries as a product of the democratization of erotic art and literature.[113] Before the advent of the printing press and widespread literacy, erotic art and literature was largely confined to the upper classes. Aristocrats and intellectuals kept and examined sexually explicit writings and paintings in "secret museums."[114] As education spread and as the new industry of printing developed,[115] money could be made by the sale of the illicit to the so-called lower classes. The ruling classes viewed this development with great alarm; they sought to regulate it, to keep erotica out of the reach of the lower classes. "In other words," Lynn Hunt writes, "pornography as a regulatory category was invented in response to the perceived menace of the democratization of culture."[116] That is, "Pornography developed out of the . . . push and pull between the intention of authors . . . to test the boundaries of the 'decent' and the aim of the . . . police to regulate it."[117] She further states:

> As Kendrick argued, the concept of pornography was historically shaped, and its development as a category was always one of conflict and change. Pornography was the name for a cultural battle zone: " 'pornography' names an argument, not a thing."[118]

From the year 1500 to the end of the French Revolution, pornography frequently was linked with political and religious change and revolution. Political and literary subversives used pornography as an effective weapon against the aristocracy, monarchy, and clergy. In France, for example, Marie Antoinette was portrayed in drawings and writings as a debauchee who gave herself to everyone, including her son. The king was depicted in explicit drawings and books as impotent and in general as a figure of sexual comedy and depravity. Similar pornographic portraits were written and painted about nobles and clergy.[119]

Women were frequently presented in pornography of this era as feisty and emancipated, but there was no real equality in gender treatment. Indeed, Hunt emphasizes: "Democracy was established against monarchy through pornographic attacks on the feminization of both the aristocracy and monarchy. It was accelerated in and after 1789 by especially vicious attacks against the leading female figure of the *ancien régime*, the queen herself."[120] Hunt concludes that "[w]omen were thus essential to the development of democracy and, in the end, excluded from it."[121] As she wrote, Julie, heroine of a famous pornographic work, passed from man to man and in the end "retired from political life to raise children and tend her garden."[122]

Granted that this theme was present, pornography in that era still contributed to the seditious concept that men and women are equal. Professor Robert Darnton writes that "carnal knowledge could open the way to enlightenment—the radical enlightenment of La Mettrie, Helvetius, Diderot, and d'Holbach."[123] The fictitious females of eighteenth-century pornography challenged the "subordination of women under the Old Regime. Above all they challenged the authority of the church, which did more than any other institution to keep women in their place. The pornography is so shot through with anticlericalism that it often seems more a matter of religion than obscenity."[124] Women are depicted as having sex with monks and bishops in contexts that make fools and hypocrites of the clergy.[125]

Darnton states that the women learn "that all men are equal, once you get them in bed. . . . But the lower classes always outdo the upper. . . . The conclusion is clear: 'In the state of nature, all men are equal.' "[126] Darnton emphasizes that the same theme applied to the status of men and women. Pornography of this century (admittedly written by men) asserted that male and female differences "came down to little or nothing, because all humans were 'machines' composed of the same tiny particles of matter."[127]

Despite these notions, much of sex depicted in these works

illustrated male dominance. Thus a "bride's virginity was a fortress to be stormed, the bed a battlefield, the deflowering a slaughter."[128] But sex was also described as a method by which women achieved a kind of spiritual and intellectual independence; after sex women gain insight into the superstitions of the clergy and the power of reason.[129]

The French Revolution marked an end to the use of pornography as a political vehicle for attacks on the regime. Political success seemed to free pornography for its modern use as a purely sexual vehicle.[130] Political freedom liberated the presses, and writers and publishers discovered they could make profits on apolitical pornography, which concentrated on the depiction of sex for sensual purposes. During this era, the ideology of a separate, private sphere for women began to develop. Traditional differences between men and women were emphasized. Yet pornography frequently dismissed the differences between the sexes in matters of sexuality.[131] Hunt argued that as "new biological and moral standards for sexual difference evolved, pornography seemed to become even more exotic and dangerous. It had to be stamped out."[132] The old regime wanted to censor pornography because of its subversive, indecent political message; newer regimes wanted to eliminate it because of its attacks on traditional notions of moral decency. In either case, pornography embodied the conflict between the commercial and artistic goals of good and bad artists, and the security and morality concerns of governmental authorities.[133]

About pornography, Professor Darnton concludes:

> The missing element in the current debate about pornography can be put as a proposition derived from Claude Levi-Strauss: sex is good for thinking. In *La Pensée sauvage* and other works, Levi-Strauss argues that many peoples do not think in the manner of philosophers, by manipulating abstractions. Instead, they think

with things—concrete things from everyday life. . . . Some things are especially good to think about. . . . Sex is not simply a subject but a tool used to pry the top off things and explore their inner works.[134]

FEMINIST OPPOSITION TO PORNOGRAPHY AS AN EXPRESSION OF MALE DOMINATION

Foucault argued that the ancient Greeks defined "proper" sex as the male playing the active role and the female the passive. In the eighteenth century, pornography was used as a weapon in a political battle against the *ancien régime*. More recently, Professor Catharine MacKinnon has argued that modern pornography is the subordination of women played out in written or visual scenes of graphic sexual behavior.[135] Whereas French revolutionaries used pornography to help eliminate what they perceived as the "feminization of the monarchy," MacKinnon would use censorship of pornography to attack the masculine domination of society. In both cases pornography is linked to politics.

For MacKinnon, pornography is a political weapon in the hands of the ruling masculine hierarchy; dismantle it, and women achieve political and social equality. Where graphic depictions of sex involve equal treatment of gender, in MacKinnon's view, it is not pornography. She and her colleague Andrea Dworkin[136] drafted the famous anti-pornography ordinance passed by Indianapolis[137] that defined pornography in terms of female subordination. The ordinance was struck down by the Court of Appeals for the Seventh Circuit on First Amendment grounds.[138]

MacKinnon comes out of an intellectual background that asserts the primacy of language.[139] She also is influenced by structuralist theories of determinism, which see human events as determined by the "hidden structures of society."[140] In

MacKinnon's view, the underlying structure is the institution of male domination, and its totalitarian control is implemented and constituted by the language of paternalism. Language is the metaphysical reality that determines the being of men and women: first there is the word, then everything else follows. Language, MacKinnon asserts, is the tool by which powerful males dominate and construct reality.[141] Thus we live in a male-dominated world, she asserts, in which the depiction of sex is almost inevitably symbolic and illustrative of the physical and spiritual hegemony of the male. Pornography is the "graphic sexually explicit subordination of women, whether in pictures or in words" by which women are dehumanized as sexual objects and, therefore, become subject to rape and mutilation.[142] Much of what MacKinnon would forbid is already covered by obscenity laws criminalizing repulsive sex, which lacks serious artistic merit. MacKinnon would, however, also ban pornography no matter how great the alleged artistic or literary value of the work, if the message is subordination of women.[143] By this definition, Shakespeare would share with the local "hard-core" porn-king the stain of pornography.

MacKinnon asserts that she is not simply arguing that pornography causes harm. Since language is the creator of our reality, the old distinctions between language and conduct are superficial.[144] The language of pornography is *itself* subordination and discrimination against women.[145] Language, MacKinnon asserts, is society, is culture, is the soul of the individual. Pornographic language is the ultimate harm. It is even more powerful than physical acts of subordination, since it reflects the bigoted "hard-wiring" of the male soul and mind.[146] Because of the power of sex itself, pornography is even more insidious than racist speech:[147] it constructs the self and society; language creates female subordination and perpetuates it; female speech is silenced, and women are rendered incapable of combatting "bad" speech with "good" speech.

Hence government censorship of pornography is essential to ending the subordination of women. Indeed, since speech is more powerful than conduct (it is a kind of conduct with a powerful ideational and emotive kick added to it), the First Amendment is perverse. That which should be *most* regulated is speech. Conduct, which is almost always derivative of speech, is less important as a governing principle of society.

Naturally, MacKinnon's emphasis on language as central to the institution of male domination is a much-disputed proposition. Wendy Kaminer writes, "I like to think words have power but I know they don't cast spells."[148] Paglia colorfully asserts that "[i]t is positively idiotic to imagine that there is no experience outside of language."[149] Professor Henry Louis Gates, Jr., eloquently argues that the "pendulum has swung from the absurd position that words don't matter to the equally absurd position that only words matter."[150] Therefore, he asserts, MacKinnon concentrates her energies on censorship rather than on campaigns to eliminate substantive inequalities.

Many feminists also dispute MacKinnon's argument because they disagree that women are always the victim.[151] Indeed, they maintain that by using the law selectively to protect women, MacKinnon's thesis tends to perpetuate women's status as victims.[152] They vigorously assert that sexual speech should be protected and that women and men should battle what they believe is harmful pornography with speech rather than censorship. Leanne Katz, executive director of the National Coalition against Censorship, argues that MacKinnon's thesis will aid the censors of the political right.[153] She points out that after MacKinnon's theories were adopted by the Canadian Supreme Court in 1992,[154] lesbian, gay, and feminist materials were banned under the "harm" standard espoused by the MacKinnon approach. Even Andrea Dworkin's books were seized, although after a media uproar they were released.

As Katz explains, "Most feminists know that campaigns to

suppress sexual expression have often been used to control *women's* sexual expression: to limit access to information about reproduction, sexual attitudes and practices, art or education."[155] In an amicus brief challenging the MacKinnon anti-pornography ordinance in Indianapolis,[156] the Feminist Anti-Censorship Task Force wrote, "The range of feminist imagination and expression in the realm of sexuality has barely begun to find voice. Women need the freedom and the socially recognized space to appropriate for themselves the robustness of what traditionally has been male language. Laws such as the one under challenge here would constrict that freedom."[157]

Judith Kegan Gardiner, professor of English and Women's Studies at the University of Illinois, describes the positive nature of pornography:

> For some women, pornography may actually deobjectify women because they can use it to validate their own desires and pleasures. They can also reinterpret or take control of the fantasy. For example they may point out that a particular pictured position is not fun, but awkward and uncomfortable. Furthermore, women too can make comparisons between their lovers and the performers, for instance to the male stars' larger organs or more sustained erections and they can use the pornography to encourage or instruct their partners how to please them.[158]

MacKinnon's analysis assumes that individuals are "malleable automatons"[159] and that individual women cannot withstand the structural forces of sexism and sexist language. Lawrence J. Siskind, a First Amendment litigator, has put it well:

> In academic circles, the concept of free will is considered quaint. Ideas have a way of filtering down from ivory towers to the rest of society.

> The jury verdicts in the Reginald Denny case were
> based, in part, on the idea that the defendants did not
> have free will, that they were caught up in the frenzy of
> violence.[160]

If human beings are simply "impressionable victims of their environment," then the First Amendment irresponsibly exposes such "receptacles to the array of exciting and disturbing influences that an unregulated environment generates."[161] Although at times humans may not think as critically as academics would hope, a concept of ourselves as blank slates lacking free will is unacceptable as a basis for banning pornography.

Perhaps the best answer to MacKinnon's powerful thesis was that of Judge Frank Easterbrook in the opinion he wrote holding the Dworkin-MacKinnon model anti-pornography law unconstitutional. He accepted for the sake of argument the law's key conclusion that portrayal of female subordination creates and institutionalizes subordination. He wrote:

> If pornography is what pornography does, so is other
> speech. . . . Efforts to suppress communist speech in the
> United States were based on the belief that the public
> acceptability of such ideas would increase the likelihood
> of totalitarian government. Religions affect socialization
> in the most pervasive way. The opinion in *Wisconsin v.*
> *Yoder* . . . shows how a religion can dominate an entire
> approach to life, governing much more than the relation
> between the sexes. Many people believe that the exis-
> tence of television, apart from the content of specific
> programs, leads to intellectual laziness, to a penchant for
> violence, to many other ills. The Alien and Sedition Acts
> passed during the administration of John Adams rested
> on a sincerely held belief that disrespect for the govern-
> ment leads to social collapse and revolution—a belief
> with support in the history of many nations. Most gov-
> ernments of the world act on this empirical regularity,

suppressing critical speech. In the United States, however, the strength of the support for this belief is irrelevant. . . .

Racial bigotry, anti-semitism, violence on television, reporters' biases—these and many more influence the culture and shape our socialization. None is directly answerable by more speech, unless that speech too finds its place in the popular culture. Yet all is protected as speech, however insidious. Any other answer leaves the government in control of all the institutions of culture, the great censor and director of which thoughts are good for us.

Sexual responses are often unthinking responses, and the association of sexual arousal with the subordination of women therefore may have a substantial effect. But almost all cultural stimuli provide unconscious responses. Religious ceremonies condition their participants. Teachers convey messages by selecting what not to cover; the implicit message about what is off limits or unthinkable may be more powerful than the messages for which they present rational argument. Television scripts contain unarticulated assumptions. People may be conditioned in subtle ways. If the fact that speech plays a role in a process of conditioning were enough to permit government regulation, that would be the end of freedom of speech.[162]

As bold as MacKinnon's analysis seems, it is not in reality different from that of censors of the past. Societies have always recognized the dangers of speech. Even before the lessons of postmodern theories of structuralism and language, societies knew of the revolutionary capabilities of speech and reacted by censoring it. Soon after Gutenberg invented the printing press and thus raised the dangers of mass distribution, officials created the first censorship bureaucracy.[163] Perhaps pornography helped bring down the French *ancien régime*; perhaps more effective censorship would have lengthened its existence. Similarly, the Spanish Inquisition argued that blasphemous speech and thought threatened the salvation of the immortal soul. Given its religious assumptions about the true faith and the value of the soul, censorship and burning were considered well worthwhile.

Certainly an immortal soul in need of saving was as important then as feminist emancipation is today. Although blasphemy may not be at the very top of the list of harmful speech in the modern industrialized Western world, in other countries it is still strongly prohibited. American conservatives in the 1940s and 1950s argued that communist speech would lead to the horrors of the totalitarian state. Given what we know now about the murderous tendencies of communist regimes, their censorious zeal was an eminently rational construct.

No government censors speech that it views as harmless. Harm is at the root of First Amendment controversy. MacKinnon has not invented a new concern. The First Amendment has bite only if it protects speech that is harmful; otherwise it is not worth the bother. For this reason, in the past the Supreme Court has ruled that "offensive" speech is protected.[164] To preserve support for the First Amendment, however, a distinction between immediate and remote harm must be made. Also, the magnitude of the harm feared should be taken into account. Finally, some distinction should be made between a harm that is unlawful—such as speech that directly results in murder—and harm that is political, social and problematical (such as the alleged harm that may result from speech that leads to protectionism).[165] If we dilute these distinctions, we merge speech with conduct (which governments always regulate based on harm concerns) and justify pervasive censorship.

The problem is not new. As Zechariah Chafee, Jr., wrote in 1949, the traditional "clear and present danger test" is designed to draw some practical line of distinction between immediate and remote harmful acts.[166] Libertarian philosophers will not convince the public, or the Court, to protect all speech, regardless of the magnitude or proximity of the harm. The recurrent problem, as Chafee said, is the "problem of Mark Anthony's Oration—discussion which is calculated to produce unlawful acts without ever mentioning them."[167] Given the types of harm society fears, the clear-and-present-danger test may fail. Walter Berns wrote in 1965:

> The first thing to be remembered [about the clear and present danger test] is that Schenk was sent to jail with it. The second is that Abrams and Gitlow, with Holmes dissenting in ringing clear and present danger language, were jailed despite it. The third is that [the communists in the Dennis case] . . . were sent to jail with it. . . . the clear and present danger test has been of assistance only to a Jehovah's Witness—not to a Socialist like Debs or a Communist like Gitlow or Dennis, or to anyone else whose views are both hated *and* feared.[168]

Today's Court, however, influenced by the *Brandenburg* doctrine, which requires a kind of immediate physical harm to trigger exceptions to the First Amendment, might have decided these cases differently. The clear-and-present-danger doctrine does not apply to obscenity law. Obscenity is not protected by the First Amendment. The harm it creates is to the traditional moral fabric of society. Obviously, this is not a discrete, immediate, unlawful, and physical kind of harm, as contemplated in *Brandenburg*.[169] It is not a specific harm to a private individual, as in the case of defamation, another exception to First Amendment protection.[170] Society so fears the culturally constructed concept of obscenity harm that legislatures ban it altogether and courts refuse to apply the clear-and-present-danger test to it.[171]

Like most censors, including supporters of obscenity censorship, MacKinnon identifies (albeit more eloquently than most) her most dreaded harm—sexual subordination of women—and argues that pornographic speech maintains and reinforces subordination. MacKinnon views the traditional obscenity doctrine as identifying a noxious, conservative notion of harm that is oblivious to the inequality of women and is embraced by a paternalistic society.[172] Conservative moralists, naturally, do not agree with that assessment. Nevertheless, their fears and hers overlap to a degree, and they agree on a fair amount—such as the Indianapolis anti-pornography ordinance.[173] Sometimes the censors' evaluations of risk of harm are correct, sometimes not. If we decide not to take that risk, we censor. The rationale of the First Amendment is that the benefit of free speech is well worth the risk.

CONCLUDING REMARKS

This brief discussion of pornography, obscenity, and eroticism cannot provide even an incomplete history of the subject. But it does begin to reveal the mystery and magic that sex plays in human life. It suggests why the Supreme Court has, from the beginning of its deliberations on the subject, placed obscenity outside the protection of the First Amendment. Sex, the Court believes, is too important to trust to the John Stuart Mill orthodoxies of free minds freely searching for the truth and individual fulfillment. That liberal mantra is acceptable for trade policy and the like, but not for the truly important subject of sex. Although some, like Justice William Brennan, would grant certain First Amendment protection to the obscene,[174] the Court as an institution has always decided that repulsive sex, lacking serious merit, is not worthy of protection. The explanation for this reluctance to protect is not based on the appeal of obscenity or pornography to the noncognitive. It is not because, as some argue, pornography is merely a masturbatory aid and not a form of expression. Almost no one, for example, doubts that the First Amendment protects hack poetry that appeals to the cheap emotions rather than to logic.

The explanation lies in the Court's fear (shared by religious conservatives) that pornography (the sexual depiction they abhor) is a particularly powerful form of expression that will create a sexual "big bang," out of which will emerge a new universe radically different from the traditional Judeo-Christian sexual culture.[175] Out of this expression will emerge, some fear, a world of homoerotic love, man-boy love, incest, sadomasochistic sex, sexual violence, and a destroyed traditional family, where Madonna will be monarch.[176] Many believe that world is already here.

Feminists like MacKinnon have a different slant—not entirely different (they fear the violence, as do conservatives), I believe, but still different. They view sex as the most important instrument of power in culture and society. As stated, MacKinnon argues that pornography is speech that creates and maintains a savage, male-dominated society. Hence, the obscene category, as legally defined, is useless, since it ignores the subordination theme. Pornography, when defined as graphic sexual expression that subordinates women, is the crucial concept and, defined as such, would chill pornographic art no matter how great the artist who creates it. Erotica that attacks the traditional family is acceptable to MacKinnon as long as it observes the principle of sexual equality. Thus MacKinnon identified a different harm from that of traditional "obscenity moralists." In both views, however, the sexual component evokes fears so great as to call (frequently with success) for censorship.

MacKinnon's argument is consistent with, indeed organically part of, the philosophy that infuses the two Supreme Court decisions on "hostile" work environments. In 1986, the Court decided that illegal sexual harassment under Title VII of the Civil Rights Act of 1964 includes conduct or speech that is "sufficiently severe or 'pervasive to alter the conditions of [the victim's] employment and create an abusive working environment.' "[177] The revolutionary concept was that "pure speech" would suffice to trigger the violation. In 1993, in its second opinion on the subject, the Court attempted to clarify that test.[178] The Court decided that female plaintiffs do not have to suffer "psychological injury" to prevail in litigation.[179]

The net result of these decisions is that an enormous hole was punched in the basic doctrine that only offensive speech is protected by the First Amendment.[180] Now, offensive speech that subjects women to male sexual domination in the workplace, if potent enough,[181] is actionable.[182] Pornography in the workplace, if it operates to discriminate against women, now receives drastically reduced First Amendment protection. Given the size of the hole punched in the ban against offensive speech, the danger is that the new doctrine may not be restrained for long to the workplace. Pornographic speech anywhere that arguably tends to reduce women to subordination or maintain them in that status is now constitutionally vulnerable to statutes that chill it. After all, if *discrimination* in employment is the acceptable mantra that validates censorship of harmful words, then words that tend to create sexual discrimination in other areas—such as in clubs, political action, the universities, art, cinema, cable television, family, etc.—may ultimately be constitutionally censorable.[183]

MacKinnon has stressed the systemic harm, as she sees it, that pornographic speech does to society and the individuals within it. Every censor, past and present, has focused on the institutional harm he or she fears and has made a similar argument for censoring the book, movie, or painting that creates that harm. It is a dangerous argument once we can constitutionally fixate on the societal harm (not crude immediate physical harm) that speech may create. It is an argument that threatens free speech, since it conflates speech with conduct.[184] Governments regulate conduct when they determine it is harmful; when we do the same with speech, we confuse it with action. Pervasive censorship then becomes inevitable.[185] The uniquely American system of free speech breaks down.

NOTES

1. Michel Foucault, 1 *The History of Sexuality: An Introduction* 35 (Robert Hurley, trans., 1990).
2. *Id.* at 78.
3. *Despite U.S. Campaign, a Boom in Pornography*, N.Y. Times, July 4, 1993, at A20.
4. *Id.*
5. *See* James Lindgren, *Defining Pornography*, 141 U. Pa. L. Rev. 1153, 1156 (1993).
6. Lynn Hunt, *Introduction, in* The Invention of Pornography 13 (Lynn Hunt, ed., 1993).
7. In an early obscenity decision, the Supreme Court asserted that sex is a "great and mysterious motive force in human life." Roth v. United States, 354 U.S. 476, 487 (1977).
8. *See* Steven G. Gey, *The Apologetics of Suppression: The Regulation of Pornography as Act and Idea*, 86 Mich. L. Rev. 1564, 1580–1 (1988); *see also* Robin West, *The Feminist-Conservative Anti-Pornography Alliance and the 1986 Attorney General's Commission on Pornography Report*, 1987 Am. B. Found. Res. J. 681 (1987).
9. Miller v. California, 413 U.S. 15, 24 (1973).
10. *See* Gey, *supra* note 8, at 1570–77. Justice Brennan, in the *Roth* obscenity case, made the morality principle clear when he pointed out (in justification for holding obscenity to be not protected) that as of 1792 all states had made blasphemy or profanity statutory crimes. *Roth*, 354 U.S. at 482–3.
11. The word is derived from the Greek *"pornographos,"* literally, "writing about prostitutes." The word first surfaced in the

Oxford English Dictionary in 1857 (Hunt, *supra* note 6, at 13) and first appeared in a 1769 French treatise called *Le Pornographe*, in reference to writing about prostitution. *Id.*

12. Hunt, *supra* note 6, at 12–3.

13. Child pornography is subject to extensive state regulation. *See* New York v. Ferber, 458 U.S. 747, 756 (1982).

14. *See* Barnes v. Glen Theatre, Inc., 501 U.S. 560 (1991); City of Renton v. Playtime Theatres, Inc., 475 U.S. 41 (1986); Young v. American Mini Theatres, Inc., 427 U.S. 50 (1976).

15. See *infra* note 177.

16. Richard A. Posner, *Sex and Reason* 355–6 (1992). The public furor greeting U.S. Surgeon General Jocelyn Elder's tentative proposal to include discussion of masturbation in the AIDS-prevention curricula of public schools indicates the strength of the taboo surrounding this topic. *See* Douglas Jehl, *Surgeon General Forced to Resign by White House*, N.Y. Times, Dec. 10, 1994, at A1.

17. Impossibly broad, that is, for certain "liberal" Western sensibilities; some conservative, "puritanical" commentators may go that far. Some feminists may ban any depiction of sex that applauds male domination.

18. Hunt, *supra* note 6, at 11.

19. Gordon Hawkins & Franklin E. Zimring, *Pornography in a Free Society* 24 (1988) (quoting Attorney General's Comm'n on Pornography, U.S. Dep't of Justice, *Final Report 227–8* (1986) [hereinafter Comm'n on Pornography]). The Meese Commission pointed out that in contrast, the term "erotica" is " 'employed to describe sexually explicit materials of which the user of the term approves.' " *Id.*

20. Chris Hedges, *Mobilizing against Pop Music and Other Horrors*, N.Y. Times, July 21, 1993, at A4.

21. *Id.*

22. Camille Paglia, *Sex, Art, and American Culture* 30 (1992).

23. Perhaps the oldest examples of pornography that have been found are ancient ivory female figures, eighteen to twenty-five thousand years old, which may be fertility symbols. John N. Wilford, *"Venus" Figurines from Ice Age Rediscovered in an Antique Shop*, N.Y. Times, Feb. 1, 1994, at C11.

24. The author agrees with the banning of child pornography. The scope of permissible regulation of child pornography is beyond the subject of this chapter.

25. Posner, *supra* note 16, at 54–66.

26. *Id*. at 55.

27. *Id*.

28. *Id*. at 56, 60–6.

29. In 1991, 68 percent of black children were born out of the marriage relationship. Charles Murray, *The Coming White Underclass*, Wall St. J., Oct. 29, 1993, at A14. The figure for white children born out of wedlock has risen to 22 percent. *Id*.

30. *See* Catharine A. MacKinnon, *Only Words* 3–8 (1993).

31. *Id*. at 7.

32. *Id*. at 114 n. 3.

33. Catharine A. MacKinnon, *A Feminist/Political Approach: Pleasure under Patriarchy, in* Theories of Human Sexuality 65, 84–5 (James H. Geer & William T. O'Donohue, eds., 1987).

34. *See* George F. Gilder, *Men and Marriage* 62–7 (1986); George F. Gilder, *Sexual Suicide* (1973).

35. *See* Daniel P. Moynihan, *Defining Deviancy Down, in* 17 Am. Scholar 62 (1993).

36. Georges Bataille, *The Accursed Share: Vol. II The History of Eroticism* 134 (Robert Hurley trans., 1991) (1976).

37. Friedrich Nietzsche, *Beyond Good and Evil* 168 (R. J. Hollingsdale, trans., 1973) (1886).

38. Bataille, *supra* note 36, at 134.

39. *Id*. at 437 n. 8.

40. Allan Bloom, *Love and Friendship* 437 (1993).

41. Posner, *supra* note 16, at 62.

42. Barry Freundel, *Two Views: Homosexuality and Halachic Judaism*, Moment, June 1993, at 40, 43. The rabbi was participating in a debate in which a non-Orthodox rabbi took issue with many aspects of his condemnation of homosexuality. *Id*.

43. *Id*. at 44.

44. Dennis Prager, *Judaism, Homosexuality and Civilization*, Moment, June 1993, at 45.

45. Moses Maimonides, *The Guide for the Perplexed* 378 (Michael Friedländer, trans., 2d ed. 1910).

46. *Id.*
47. *Id.* at 373.
48. *Id.* at 376.
49. *Id.*
50. *Id.* at 379.
51. *Id.*
52. Posner, *supra* note 16, at 48.
53. *Id.* at 49.
54. *Id.*
55. *See* Alice S. Alexiou, *The Jewish Community Uncomfortably Confronts Homosexuality*, Moment, June 1993, at 28–35.
56. Gilder, Men and Marriage, *supra*, note 34, 39–47. Maimonides, in effect, made this argument. *See supra* notes 45–51 and accompanying text.
57. Gilder, Wealth and Poverty 70–1 (1981).
58. Recently, President Clinton gave a speech before the National Baptist Church Convention in which he addressed the need to repair the nation's social fabric. To combat the rise in violence, the increasing number of children born out of wedlock, and the large percentage of pregnancies terminated in abortion, the president emphasized the need for a new, less tolerant attitude toward illegitimacy, abortion, and single parenthood. He stated that the nation would be "better off" if more people were in a "stable, traditional family." Michael Vines, *In Baptist Talk, Clinton Stresses Moral Themes*, N.Y. Times, Sept. 10, 1994, at A1.
59. *See generally*, Michel Foucault, 3 *The History of Sexuality: The Care of Self* (Robert Hurley, trans., 1988) [hereinafter Foucault, *Self*]; Michel Foucault, 2 *The History of Sexuality: The Use of Pleasure* (Robert Hurley, trans., 1990) [hereinafter Foucault, *Pleasure*].
60. The Greeks had similar attitudes toward diet; indeed, they considered the two very similar in the sense that both areas required discipline and moderation. Foucault, *Self, supra* note 59, at 141; Foucault, *Pleasure, supra* note 59, at 51.
61. Foucault, *Pleasure, supra* note 59, at 44–5.
62. *Id.* at 46–47.
63. *Id.* at 47.

64. *Id.* at 80–6.
65. *Id.* at 45.
66. *Id.* at 46.
67. *Id.*
68. *Id.* at 220.
69. *Id.* at 46.
70. Foucault, *Self,* *supra* note 59, at 24–5.
71. *Id.* at 23.
72. Foucault, *Pleasure,* *supra* note 59, at 220–1.
73. *Id.* at 224–5.
74. *Id.* at 241–2.
75. *Id.* at 242–6.
76. Certainly, Aristophanes emphasized the heterosexual nature of the ancient Greeks. His women brought an end to war by withholding their love in his play *Lysistrata.* The women in that great play seem more like the powerful women Camille Paglia describes than the mechanistic individuals Michel Foucault evokes. *See* Aristophanes, *Lysistrata* (Douglass Parker, trans., 1964).
77. Foucault, *Pleasure,* *supra* note 59, at 195.
78. *Id.* at 194.
79. *Id.* at 187–8.
80. *Id.* at 154–7.
81. *Id.* at 152–7.
82. *Id.* at 164–5.
83. Foucault, *Self,* *supra* note 59, at 189–92.
84. *Id.* at 209–10.
85. *Id.* at 148–9.
86. *Id.* at 107, 113.
87. Paglia, *supra* note 22, at 182.
88. *Id.*
89. *Id.*
90. *Id.*
91. *Id.*
92. *Id.*
93. *Id.*
94. *Id.* at 230.
95. *Id.*
96. Professor Joan Breton Connelly of New York University has

recently advanced a startling new theory of the famous Parthenon frieze, one that has gained the interest of classical scholars. She argues that the frieze (the central monument of classical culture) celebrates the heroism of women. This interpretation challenges the view that Athens was a misogynistic society. *See* Steven Coates, *A Feminist Theory of Greece's Parthenon Frieze*, Wall St. J., Jan. 6, 1994, at A10.

97. Jürgen Habermas, *Some Questions Concerning the Theory of Power: Foucault Again, in* The Philosophical Discourse of Modernity 266, 291 (Frederick Lawrence, trans., 1987).

98. Jean-François Revel, *Democracy against Itself: The Future of the Democratic Impulse* 94 (Roger Kaplan, trans., 1993).

99. Bloom, *supra* note 40, at 444.

100. *Id.* at 443.

101. *Id.* at 442.

102. Iris Murdoch, *Metaphysics as a Guide to Morals* 342–6 (1992).

103. Jürgen Habermas, *Between Eroticism and General Economics: Georges Bataille, in* The Philosophical Discourse of Modernity, *supra* note 97, at 211, 233.

104. Bataille, *supra* note 36, at 134.

105. Habermas, *supra* note 103, at 232.

106. *Id.*

107. Bataille, *supra* note 36, at 134.

108. *Id.*

109. *Id.* at 104.

110. *Id.* Indeed, eroticism is connected in some mysterious manner to primitive anxieties and taboos about death. The death of the old paves the way for the emergence of the young, and sex is involved in the transmission of new life to replace the dying. *Id.* at 97–101.

111. Habermas, *supra* note 103, at 231.

112. Id. at 232–5.

113. Hunt, *supra* note 6, at 10–4.

114. *Id.* at 12 (citing Walter Kendrick, *The Secret Museum: Pornography in Modern Culture* [1987]).

115. Soon after Gutenberg developed the press, pornography made use of the new technology. A book of "erotic engravings"

was published in 1524 and censored by the pope. John Tierney, *Porn, the Low-Slung Engine of Progress*, N.Y. Times, Jan. 9, 1994, § 2, at 18. Tierney describes how pornography has quickly exploited advances in media technology. One of the first motion pictures, an Edison movie, was named "The Kiss." *Id.* In 1978 and 1979, over 75 percent of videocassettes sold were pornographic. *Id.* Interactive computer technologies promise a new resource for the ultimate in pornographic experience. *Id.*

116. Hunt, *supra* note 6, at 12–3.

117. *Id.* at 10.

118. *Id.* at 13.

119. Lynn Hunt, *Pornography and the French Revolution, in* The Invention of Pornography, *supra* note 6, at 301, 302.

120. *Id.* at 329.

121. *Id.*

122. *Id.*

123. Robert Darnton, *Sex for Thought*, XLI The N. Y. Rev. of Books 65, 67 (Dec. 22, 1994).

124. *Id.* at 67.

125. *Id.*

126. *Id.* at 68.

127. *Id.*

128. *Id.* at 69.

129. *Id.*

130. As Hunt put it, "Pornography would continue to have political and social meanings, as it still has [,] . . . but these would now be much less intentional and much more subtle. . . ." Hunt, *supra* note 6, at 339.

131. Kathryn Norberg, *The Libertine Whore: Prostitution in French Pornography from Margot to Juliette, in* The Invention of Pornography, *supra* note 6, at 225, 251.

132. Hunt, *supra* note 6, at 45.

133. *Id.* at 10.

134. Darnton, *supra* note 123 at 65.

135. MacKinnon, *supra* note 30, at 20–7.

136. *See* Andrea Dworkin, Pornography: *Men Possessing Women* (3d ed. 1981).

137. *See* Donald A. Downs, *The New Politics of Pornography* 95–143 (1989).

138. American Booksellers Ass'n v. Hudnut, 771 F. 2d 323 (7th Cir. 1985), *aff'd*, 475 U.S. 1001 (1986). The ordinance, in part, defined pornography as "the graphic sexually explicit subordination of women, whether in pictures or words." *Id.* at 324.

139. *See* Jürgen Habermas, *Beyond a Temporalized Philosophy of Origins: Jacques Derrida's Critique of Phonocentrism, in* The Philosophical Discourse of Modernity, *supra* note 103, at 161.

140. Paul Johnson, *Modern Times: The World from the Twenties to the Eighties* 695 (1983).

141. *See generally* MacKinnon, *supra* note 30.

142. *American Booksellers*, 771 F.2d at 324 (quoting from the Indianapolis version of the MacKinnon/Dworkin anti-pornography ordinance).

143. MacKinnon, *supra* note 30, at 22.

144. *Id.* at 21–2.

145. In this regard her position has received general support from the Supreme Court. *See* Harris v. Forklift Systems, Inc., 114 S. Ct. 367 (1993) (abusive speech in the workplace may constitute illegal discrimination under Title VII of the Civil Rights Act).

146. MacKinnon, *supra* note 30, at 61.

147. *Id.* at 61–2.

148. National Coalition against Censorship, *The Sex Panic: Women, Censorship and "Pornography"* 7 (1993) [hereinafter *The Sex Panic*].

149. Paglia, *supra* note 22, at 214.

150. Henry L. Gates, Jr., *Is the First Amendment Racist?: Why Civil Liberties Pose No Threat to Civil Rights*, New Republic, Sept. 20, 1993, at 37–49.

151. *See* Hawkins & Zimring, *supra* note 19, at 167–8.

152. *See* The Sex Panic, *supra* note 148, at 6–9.

153. Leanne Katz, *Censors' Helpers*, N.Y. Times, Dec. 4, 1993, at A21.

154. Butler v. Her Majesty, 89 D.L.R. 4th 449 (Can. 1992).

155. Katz, *supra* note 153, at 21.

156. American Booksellers Ass'n v. Hudnut, 771 F.2d 323, (7th Cir. 1985), *aff'd*, 475 U.S. 1001 (1986).

157. Nat Hentoff, *Free Speech for Me—But Not for Thee* 352 (1992).

158. Judith K. Gardiner, *What I Didn't Get to Say about Por-*

nography, Masculinity, and Repression, in New York Law Review Symposium: The Sex Panic, as quoted in Nadine Strossen, *Defending Pornography* 166 (1995).

159. Lawrence J. Siskind, *The Folly and Futility of Censoring Violence*, Legal Times, Nov. 22, 1993, at 28, 29.

160. *Id.* at 29.

161. *Id.*

162. American Booksellers Association v. Hudnut, 771 F.2d 323, 329–30 (7th Cir. 1985), *aff'd*, 475 U.S. 1001 (1986).

163. Rodney A. Smolla, *Free Speech in an Open Society* 338 (1992).

164. *See, e.g.*, Cohen v. California, 403 U.S. 15 (1971).

165. The Meese Commission argued that aggressive forms of pornography have a relationship to sexually violent behavior. Two researchers who had been cited by the Commission stated:

> "Despite the [Meese Commission's] report that most forms of pornography have a causal relationship to sexually aggressive behavior, we find it difficult to understand how this conclusion was reached. . . .
>
> "Most social scientists who testified before the commission were also cautious . . . when making statements about causal links between pornography and sexually aggressive behavior. *Any reasonable view of the research would not come to the conclusion . . . that pornography conclusively results in antisocial effects.*"

Hentoff, *supra* note 157, at 347. *See also* Nadine Strossen, *Defending Pornography*, ch. 12 (1995) (discussing the lack of connection between pornography and harm to women).

166. Zechariah Chafee, Jr., *Book Review*, 62 Harv. L. Rev. 891, 898–9 (1949) (reviewing Alexander Meiklejohn, *Free Speech and Its Relation to Self-Government* [1948]).

167. *Id.* at 899.

168. Walter Berns, *Freedom, Virtue and the First Amendment* 50–56 (1965) as quoted in Steven H. Shiffrin and Jesse H. Choper, *The First Admendment, Cases—Comments—Questions*, at 75 n.b. (2d ed., 1996).

169. Brandenburg v. Ohio, 395 U.S. 444 (1969).

170. *See* New York Times Co. v. Sullivan, 376 U.S. 255 (1964).

171. *See* Miller v. California, 413 U.S. 15 (1973).

172. MacKinnon, *supra* note 30, at 87–91.

173. Downs, *supra* note 137, at 95–143.

174. *See* Paris Adult Theatre I v. Slaton, 413 U.S. 49, 83, 94, 111 (1973) (Brennan, J., dissenting); *see also Miller*, 413 U.S. at 48.

175. In *Paris Adult Theatre I*, then–Chief Justice Burger upheld a ban on obscene movies: "[T]here is a 'right of the Nation and of the States to maintain a decent society.' " 413 U.S. at 59–60 (quoting Jacobellis v. Ohio, 378 U.S. 184, 199 [1964] [Warren, C.J., dissenting]). He also quoted Professor Bickel: "It concerns the tone of the society, the mode, or to use terms that have perhaps greater currency, the style and quality of life, now and in the future." *Id.* at 59.

176. In Barnes v. Glen Theatre, Inc., 501 U.S. 560 (1991), Chief Justice Rehnquist, delivering the judgment of the Court, stated: "The traditional police power of the States is defined as the authority to provide for the public health, safety, and morals. . . . In *Paris Adult Theatre I v. Slaton*, we said:

> 'In deciding [Roth v. United States, 354 U.S. 476 (1957)], this Court implicitly accepted that a legislature could legitimately act on such a conclusion to protect "the social interest in order and morality." ' '

Id. at 569.

177. Meritor Savings Bank v. Vinson, 477 U.S. 57, 67 (1986) (quoting Hensen v. Duretees, 682 F.2d 897, 904 [1982]). Title VII of the Civil Rights Act of 1964 makes it "an unlawful employment practice for an employer . . . to discriminate against any individual with respect to his compensation, terms, conditions or privileges of employment, because of such individual's race, color, religion, sex or national origin." 42 U.S.C. § 2000e-2(a) (1). *Meritor* made it clear that the statutory language encompasses harassing, sexually discriminatory speech.

178. Harris v. Fork Lift Sys., Inc., 114 S. Ct. 367 (1993).

179. *Id.* at 370–1.

180. Jeffrey Rosen, *Fast Food Justice*, N.Y. Times, Nov. 16, 1993, at A27.

181. The Court stated that there cannot be "a mathematically precise test." *Harris*, 114 S. Ct. at 371. The factors include "frequency," "severity," "whether it is physically threatening or humiliating, or a mere offensive utterance," and "whether it unreasonably interferes with an employee's work performance." *Id.*

182. Justice Scalia criticized the test as inherently vague but could do no better. *Id.* at 372 (Scalia, J., concurring).

183. *See, e.g.*, Franklin v. Gwinnett County Pub. Sch., 112 S. Ct. 1028 (1992) (applying Title VI or Title VII–type damages in a Title IX suit); Grove City College v. Bell, 465 U.S. 555, 566 (1984) (finding Title IX requirements did not infringe First Amendment rights of the college).

184. For a very thoughtful piece on the topic of harassment, see Eugene Volokh, *Freedom of Speech and Workplace Harassment*, 39 UCLA L. Rev. 1791, 1863–71 (1992).

185. *See generally* Jonathan Rauch, *Kindly Inquisitors: The New Attacks on Free Thought* (1993).

CHAPTER 6

CONCLUSION

In the end, the arguments of the new critics of traditional liberal defenses of the First Amendment turn on power. Elite white groups possess power; subjugated minority groups and women lack power. Speech is merely the epiphenomenon of power, to use the language of the older Marxist left. Free speech is merely a cunning device by which the dominant hierarchies cultivate and preserve their dominance. Culture, books, plays, cinema, history, and philosophy are products of the ruling elites. They possess no truth or value outside of their instrumental value to the elites. It is a grim world.

They argue that law (including First Amendment doctrine) is merely the product of power-group lobbying and influence. The very scope of First Amendment doctrine turns and twists with the influence of interest-group politicking. Ideas of truth, democracy, beauty, autonomy, or legal reasoning are largely irrelevant (or more accurately, radically subjective), at least until the right group, namely the new critics, reach power. Thus First Amendment doctrine is viewed as merely the product of lobbying and maneuvering of groups whose economic interest will be satisfied by new twists in the doctrine. The more powerful the group, the more certainly it will get the proper constitutional doctrine.

The new critics agree, then, that speech, argument, reason, or emotion have little influence independent of the power of elite groups at the top of the power structure. This is a despairing vision of society. It is nihilistic and cynical to its core. It fundamentally eschews word, book, and idea as elements of society. In the final analysis, it is radically more deeply skeptical than the methodological skepticism that, as I discussed in Chapter 2, underlies traditional First Amendment doctrine. It is a movement that is systemically cynical about the value of discourse. It is a philosophy that denies the value of human conversation. In order to rescue itself from total nihilism, it rather arbitrarily asserts that there is no truth anywhere, *except* in the assertions of certain minority and pro-censorship groups: those organizations, ironically, *do* possess objective truth. Since the sole basis for denial of the present culture is the assertion that it is based on power, the new ordering, which will be based on a new power structure, is also devoid of truth. But the new critics deny that their power is subject to criticism. Shakespeare, Locke, Jefferson, and Western civilization itself will be dethroned, to be replaced by a new power structure that will be valid and worthwhile, notwithstanding the corrosive skepticism and cynicism that underlies the new critics' approach to the values of our culture.

The new thinking, if successful, will decisively end the free exchange of ideas that underlies all of Western culture and civilization, or indeed all cultures. Race, ethnicity, and gender will be the sole determinants of the university and the media. Because ideas are useless, because they are in reality the disguised weapons of power and have no independent validity, all discourse turns into warfare. Because legal briefs on a First Amendment case are irrelevant, the only thing for the so-called scholar to do is to measure the pocketbook and power of the litigant. This approach makes dreamy-eyed idealists out of the old legal realists. The judicial process is otherwise irrelevant. Likewise, all art and literature is to be evaluated on the basis of the race and wealth of the author or of his or her patrons. Such a recipe, now embraced by so many in the academy, is a recipe for the end of discourse and of the world of ideas and culture.

The free speech principle is closely linked, it is clear, to the kind of society we desire. The First Amendment envisages a democratic, vigorous culture in which discourse significantly affects the shape of society. More effective writers, more effective newspaper owners and editors will win the day. The results will not be to the liking of the losers in this competition. I, for one, deplore the success of Patrick Buchanan as a syndicated columnist, television commentator, and politician. At one point, his verbal assault on the Jews and Israel led A. Rosenthal of the *New York Times* criticize him severely.[1] Although I might, in a weak moment, desire a structure that censored Buchanan, I believe that the only safe system for liberty and freedom is the one we have, in which answers to Buchanan must come from other writers and politicians, not the state.

This is not to deny—it would be foolish—that disparities in birth and wealth do not have an impact on the power of speech. Readers of this book share free speech with the owners of the *New York Times*, but obviously, patently, the latter have more speech than do our readers and this author. In this book, however, we have attempted to demonstrate that state censorship or channeling of speech is a dangerous weapon to use to address those issues of inequality.

I do not wish to give the impression from the past few paragraphs that speech alone is the determinant of success or failure of disparate groups in society. We can overemphasize the influence of speech. We saw a dramatic example of this in Eastern Europe, where decades of communist control of speech and propaganda against religion, nationalism, and ethnicity broke down almost overnight, to reveal that ethnic differences, ethnic rivalries, religious beliefs, and nationalism had not been dissolved by the years of speech control. Complex patterns of culture, not yet successfully analyzed by science, explain differences among groups.

The First Amendment has often been justified as a method or means for facilitating the democratic process. On one level, this is a fairly tautological proposition. Democracy entails the competition of rival groups and individuals, and the settlement of disputes by periodic votes. Since speech is the medium by which differences are aired and debated, freedom of speech is a kind of synonym for the democratic system. It is difficult to imagine a vote in Congress, or an election, in the total absence of free speech, unless we wish to mimic the elections in Nazi Germany or Stalin's Russia. Speech has also been justified as a safety valve for discontent that permits a democratic society to evolve without violence.

On a deeper level, the free speech principle, in conjunction with the democratic process, helps create a certain kind of society. It entails a society in constant flux and dynamic change. Nothing is fixed, nothing is taken for granted. The marketplace of ideas is a dynamic process of movement and turmoil; change is the only constant. Although free speech is perhaps not necessary for a successful free-enterprise system, it has certainly been a characteristic of modern market economies. Capitalism is distinct from other bases of societies— feudal, socialist, or religious fundamentalist—in the force and rapidity of change and movement.[2] Capitalism is constantly destroying the old and creating the new. Technology and free enterprise produce the cinema, and the world changes. Entrepreneurs develop the internal combustion engine, and the face of the earth changes. The same occurs in the world of ideas, speech, art, and the newspaper.

Some thirty years ago, explicit sex was taboo in the cinema, Victorian sexual mores were not yet in tatters, and women at a college lived in separate dorms and observed fixed evening hours of residence. All that has changed, due largely to the influence of free speech in the form of cinema, magazine, book, and speech, along with the influence of the pill, and a host of other causes. Such a society has its costs. There are winners and losers. There is constant motion, stress, and conflict. But there is also freedom and autonomy, prosperity and initiative.

As mentioned, market economies and free speech are frequently present together. The free flow of information, ideas, and technology is essential in the modern age. We live in an age of information. The Internet, computer, microchip, fax, television, and cinema have created a universe in which the barriers to information and new ideas fail everywhere. It is no accident that communism as a living ideology collapsed as this age came to fruition. Communist systems were unable to compete with the new technologies and economies based upon the computer. The explosive mix of free speech, fax machines, and computers has created a universal knowledge and appreciation of the achievements of democracy and capitalism. Students in China, before the regime murdered them, marched with Statues of Liberty and slogans based upon the Jeffersonian ideals of the American Revolution.

The new critics stress the value of equality above all other values. Only an authoritarian or totalitarian state can impose that goal. Only the state can place all individuals and all groups in a position of equality with all other groups. To do that, more successful groups or individuals must be restrained in speech as well as conduct. Interest group politics are suspect, and would be ended. Authoritarian or totalitarian states can accomplish those results; a strong libertarian version of the First Amendment is a threat to that goal. The new critics view free speech as a wild card that has created uncertain, unpredictable, and unequal results. Hence, they desire to dampen spontaneous change and create a fixed, static society.

But their efforts will fail, because of the difficulties in the modern age of fax machines and the World Wide Web, to restrain the speech they detest. Disfavored speech would be driven underground, but it would subsist. The result, as Thomas Emerson indicated in an earlier time, would be to magnify the possibilities of resentment and violence.[3] Indeed, the state censorship of hateful language, and more important, the subtle variations thereof, would have a contrary effect. The forbidden would gain a sort of attractiveness.

The traditional liberal vision of the First Amendment enhances the speech power of minorities—gays, lesbians, African-Americans, and women. The Supreme Court has applied the First Amendment to protect the speech of minorities, as well as the internal governance structures of minority associations which are vehicles of free speech.[4] Thus the Court bars government interference with the democratic processes of private groups. The Court has used this approach to safeguard minority group organizations from the excesses of an intolerant government.

This is a liberal, free speech way to advance the opportunity of minorities to move forward, on their own initiatives, in the American culture. Alexis de Tocqueville recognized long ago that it is, in the words of Justice Anthony Kennedy, "a distinctive part of the American character for individuals to join associations to enrich the public dialogue."[5] Justice Kennedy quotes de Tocqueville as follows: "Americans of all ages, all conditions, and all dispositions constantly form associations. . . . If it is proposed to inculcate some truth, or to foster some feeling by the encouragement of a great example, they form a society."[6]

Hence, the First Amendment facilitates the ability of minority groups and feminists to organize, to establish their own organizational rules and standards for membership, to agitate, to march, and to demonstrate, in order to change society. The same freedom permits religious fundamentalists to organize and seek power. The new critics do not fully trust the marketplace in speech and ideas to accomplish the proper result.

Indeed, they are concerned that speech they dislike may succeed. It was a similar fear that led government to ban free speech for millennia.

NOTES

1. Joshua Muravchik, *Patrick J. Buchanan and the Jews*, 91 Commentary, Jan. 1991, at 29.

2. *See e.g.*, Michael Novak, *The Spirit of Democratic Capitalism*, ch. IX (1982); Joseph Schumpeter, *Capitalism, Socialism, and Democracy* 146 (3d ed. 1975).

3. Thomas Emerson, *The System of Freedom of Expression* 6–7 (1970).

4. *See* discussion of cases and issues in Roberts v. United States Jaycees, 468 U.S. 609 (1984).

5. Austin v. Michigan Chamber of Commerce, 111 S. Ct. 1391, 1424 (1990).

6. *Id.* (quoting 2 Alexis de Tocqueville, *Democracy in America* 106 (P. Bradley, ed., 1948).

BIBLIOGRAPHY

Abrams, Kathryn, *Gender Discrimination and the Transformation of Workplace Norms*, 42 Vand. L. Rev. 1183 (1989).

Academic Groups Fighting the 'Politically Correct Left' Gain Momentum, Chron. of Higher Educ., Dec. 12, 1990 at A-3.

Alexander, Edward, *A Talmud for Americans*, 90 Commentary, July 1990, at 27.

Alexander, L., *Low Value Speech*, 83 Nw. U.L. Rev. 547 (1989).

Alexiou, Alice S., *The Jewish Community Uncomfortably Confronts Homosexuality*, Moment, June 1993, at 28–35.

Aristophanes, *Lysistrata* (Douglass Parker, trans., University of Michigan Press, 1964).

Bataille, Georges, *The Accursed Share: Vol. II The History of Eroticism* (Robert Hurley, trans., Zone Books 1991) (1976).

Becker, Mary E., *The Politics of Women's Wrongs and the Bill of "Rights": A Bicentennial Perspective*, 59 U. Chi. L. Rev. 453, (1992).

Berke, Richard, *Ethics Unit Singles Out Cranston, Chides 4 Others in S & L Inquiry*, N.Y. Times, Feb. 28, 1991, at 1.

Berlin, Isaiah, *Four Essays on Liberty* (Oxford University Press, 1969).

Berns, Walter, *Freedom, Virtue and the First Amendment* (H. Regnery, 1965).

Bloom, Allen, *Giants and Dwarfs* (Simon & Schuster, 1990).

———, *Love & Friendship* (Simon & Schuster, 1993).

Bork, Robert, *Neutral Principles and Some First Amendment Problems*, 47 Ind. L. J. I (1971).

Chafee, Zechariah, Jr., *Book Review*, 62 Harv. L. Rev. 891 (1949).

Darnton, Robert, *Sex for Thought*, XLI The New York Review of Books 65 (Dec. 22, 1994).

Davidowicz, Lucy, *How They Teach the Holocaust*, 90 Commentary, Dec. 1990, at 25.

Delgado, Richard, *Campus Antiracism Rules: Constitutional Narratives in Collision*, 85 Nw. U.L. Rev. 343 (1991).

———, *Professor Delgado Replies*, 18 Harv. C.R.-C.L. L. Rev. 592 (1983).

———, *Words That Wound: A Tort Action for Racial Insults, Epithets, and Name-Calling*, 17 Harv. C.R.-C.L. L. Rev. 133 (1982).

Dennett, Daniel C., *Denying Darwin, David Berlinski, and Critics*, 102 Commentary, Sept. 1996, at 6.

Derrida, Jacques, *Of Grammatology* (Gayatri Chakravorty, trans, The Johns Hopkins University Press, 1976).

Despite U.S. Campaign, a Boom in Pornography, N.Y. Times, July 4, 1993, at A20.

Dewey, John, *Experience and Nature* (Open Court Publishing Co., 1926).

Diggins, John P., *The Promise of Pragmatism* (The University of Chicago Press, 1994).

Downs, Donald A., *The New Politics of Pornography* (The University of Chicago Press, 1989).

D'Souza, Dinesh, *Illiberal Education: The Politics of Race and Sex on Campus* (Free Press, 1991).

Dworkin, Andrea, *Pornography: Men Possessing Women* (Women's Press, 3d ed. 1981).

Dworkin, Andrea, and Catharine A. MacKinnon, *Pornography and Civil Rights: A New Day for Women's Equality* (Organizing Against Pornography, 1988).

Ehrenreich, Nancy S., *Pluralist Myths and Powerful Men: The Ideology of Reasonableness in Sexual Harassment Law*, 99 Yale L. J. 1177 (1990).

Emerson, Thomas, *The System of Freedom of Expression* (Random House, 1970).

Estrich, Susan, *Sex at Work*, 43 Stan. L. Rev. 813 (1991).

Fitzjames, S., *Liberty, Equality, Fraternity* (London: Smith, Elder, 1874).

Forer, L. G., *A Chilling Effect: The Mounting Threat of Libel and Invasion of Privacy Actions to the First Amendment* (W. W. Norton & Co., 1987).

Foucault, Michel 1 *The History of Sexuality: An Introduction* (Robert Hurley, trans., Vintage Books, 1990).

————, 2 *The History of Sexuality: The Use of Pleasure* (Robert Hurley, trans., Vintage Books, 1990).

————, 3 *The History of Sexuality: The Care of Self* (Robert Hurley, trans., Vintage Books, 1988).

France, Steve, *Hate Goes to College*, 76 A. B. A. J., July 1990, at 44.

Freundel, Barry, *Two Views: Homosexuality and Halachic Judaism*, Moment, June 1993, at 40.

Gallucci, Ed, *A Gathering Storm over the Politically Correct*, Newsweek, Dec. 24, 1990, at 48.

Gates, Henry L., Jr., *Is the First Amendment Racist? Why Civil Liberties Pose No Threat to Civil Rights*, New Republic, Sept. 20, 1993 at 37.

Gey, Steven G., *The Apologetics of Suppression: The Regulation of Pornography as Act and Idea*, 86 Mich. L. Rev. 1564 (1988).

Gilder, George F., *Men & Marriage* (Pelican Publishing Co., 1986).

————, *Sexual Suicide* (Quadrangle Press, 1973).

————, *Wealth & Poverty* (Bantam Books, 1981).

Givelber, David, *The Right to Minimum Social Decency and the Limits of Evenhandedness: Intentional Infliction of Emotional Distress by Outrageous Conduct*, 82 Colum. L. Rev. 42, 46 (1982).

Goings On About Town: The Theatre, The New Yorker (Nov. 19, 1990), at 4.

Greenawalt, Kent, *Insults and Epithets: Are They Protected Speech?* 42 Rutgers L. Rev. 287 (1990).

Gunther, Gerald, *Individual Rights in Constitutional Law* 754 (The Foundation Press, 5th ed. 1992).

———, *Learned Hand the Man and the Judge* (Alfred A. Knopf, 1994).

Habermas, Jürgen, *The Philosophical Discourse of Modernity* (Frederick G. Lawrence, trans., The MIT Press, 1987).

Haiman, Franklyn S., *Speech Acts and the First Amendment* (Southern Illinois University Press, 1993).

Halloran, Richard, *Hawaii Journal: Rare Storm over Race Ruffles a Mixed Society*, N.Y. Times, Dec. 26, 1990, at A20.

Harsthorne, Charles & Paul Weiss, eds., *Collected Papers of Charles Sanders Peirce, Vol. 5, Pragmatism and Pragmaticism* (Harvard University Press, 1965).

Hawkins, G., & F. E. Zimring, *Pornography In a Free Society* (Cambridge University Press, 1988).

Hedges, Chris, *Mobilizing against Pop Music and Other Horrors*, N.Y. Times, July 21, 1993, at A4.

Heins, Marjorie, *Banning Words: A Comment on "Words That Wound,"* 18 Harv. C.R.-C.L. L. Rev. 585 (1983).

Hentoff, Nat, *Free Speech for Me—But Not for Thee* (HarperCollins Publishers, 1992).

———, *"Speech Codes" on the Campus and Problems of Free Speech*, *in* Debating P. C. 215 (Paul Berman, ed., Dell Publishing, 1992).

Holmes, Stephen, *The Anatomy of Antiliberalism* (Harvard University Press, 1993).

Hunt, Lynn, ed., *The Invention of Pornography* (Zone Books, 1993).

James, William, *The Will to Believe*, first published in 1897 (Longmans, Green & Co., 1927).

Jehl, Douglas, *Surgeon General Forced to Resign by White House*, N.Y. Times, Dec. 10, 1994, at A1.

Johnson, Paul, *Modern Times: The World from the Twenties to the Eighties* (Harper & Row Publishers, 1983).

Katz, Jacob, *The Darker Side of Genius: Richard Wagner's Anti-Semitism* (Brandeis University Press, 1986).

Katz, Leanne, *Censors' Helpers*, N.Y. Times, Dec. 4, 1993, at A21.

Kaus, Mickey, *Mickey Kaus Skewers Wm. F. Buckley*, The New Republic, Dec. 31, 1990, at 34.

Kirkpatrick, Jeane J., *How the PLO Was Legitimized*, 88 Commentary, July 1989.

Kretzmer, David, *Freedom of Speech and Racism*, 8 Cardozo L. Rev. 445 (1987).

Lasch, Christopher, *The Revolt of the Elites* (W. W. Norton & Co., 1995).

Lawrence, Charles R., *If He Hollers Let Him Go: Regulating Racist Speech on Campus*, 1990 Duke L. J., 431, 438–49 (1990).

Leff, Arthur, *Economic Analysis of Law: Some Realism about Nominalism*, 60 Va. L. Rev. 451 (1974).

Levy, Leonard, *Emergence of a Free Press* (Oxford University Press, 1985).

Lindgren, James, *Defining Pornography*, 141 U. Pa. L. Rev. 1153 (1993).

MacKinnon, Catharine A., *A Feminist/Political Approach: Pleasure under Patriarchy, in* Theories of Human Sexuality (James H. Geer & William T. O'Donohue, eds., Plenum Press, 1987).

———, *Only Words* (Harvard University Press, 1993).

———, *Pornography, Civil Rights, and Speech*, 20 Harv. C.R.-C.L. L. Rev. 1 (1985).

Maimonides, Moses, *The Guide for the Perplexed* (Michael Friedländer, trans., George Routledge & Sons Ltd., 2d ed. 1910).

Markham, Ian S., *Plurality & Christian Ethics* (Cambridge University Press, 1994).

Marx, Karl, *On the Jewish Question* (Hebrew Union College, Jewish Institute of Religion, 1958) (1844).

Matsuda, Mari J., *Public Response to Racist Speech: Considering the Victim's Story*, 87 Mich. L. Rev. 2320 (1989).

Matthews, Anne, *Deciphering Victorian Underwear and Other Seminars*, N.Y. Times, Feb. 10, 1991 (Magazine), at 42.

McChesney, Fred S., *A Positive Regulatory Theory of the First Amendment*, 20 Conn. L. Rev 355 (1988).

Meiklejohn, Alexander, *Free Speech and Its Relation to Self-Government* (Harper, 1948).

Meyer, Michael A., *Anti-Semitism and Jewish Identity*, 88 Commentary, Nov. 1989, at 35.

Mill, John Stuart, *On Liberty* (D. Spitz, ed., W. W. Norton & Co., 1975).

Moynihan, Daniel P., *Defining Deviancy Down*, 17 Am. Scholar 62 (1993).

Muravchik, Joshua, *Patrick J. Buchanan and the Jews*, 91 Commentary, Jan. 1991, at 29.

Murdoch, I., *Metaphysics as a Guide to Morals* (The Penguin Press, 1992).

Murray, Charles, *The Coming White Underclass*, Wall St. J., Oct. 29, 1993, at A14.

Neuhaus, Richard J., *The Ambiguities of "Christian America."* Concordia Journal 291–2 (July 1991).

———, *The Naked Public Square: Religion and Democracy in America*, (W. B. Eerdmans Pub. Co., 2d ed. 1995, originally published 1984).

———, *Why We Can Get Along*, 60 First Things 27 (Feb. 1966).

Nietzsche, Friedrich, *Beyond Good and Evil* (R. J. Hollingdale, trans., Penguin, 1973) (1886).

Novak, Michael, *The Spirit of Democratic Capitalism* (Simon & Schuster, 1982).

Nowak, John, et al., *Constitutional Law* (West Publishing Co., 3d ed. 1986).

Paglia, Camille, *Sex, Art, and American Culture* (Vintage Books, 1992).

Pangle, Thomas L., *The Enabling of Democracy* (The Johns Hopkins University Press, 1992).

Plato, *The Republic in* The Portable Plato (S. Buchanan, ed., Penguin Books, 1977).

Posner, Richard, *Law and Literature: A Misunderstood Relation* (Harvard University Press, 1989).

———, *The Problems of Jurisprudence* (Harvard University Press, 1990).

———, *Sex and Reason* (Harvard University Press, 1992).

———, *What Has Pragmatism to Offer Law?*, 63 S. Cal. Rev. 1653 (1990).

Post, Robert C., *Racist Speech, Democracy, and the First Amendment in* Speaking of Race, Speaking of Sex 146 (New York University Press, 1994).

Prager, Dennis, *Judaism, Homosexuality and Civilization*, Moment, June 1993, at 45.

Putnam, Hilary, *Renewing Philosophy* (Harvard University Press, 1992).

————, *Words and Life* (Harvard University Press, 1994).

Race on Campus, New Republic, Feb. 18, 1991 at 5–6, 18–47, 49–53.

Ratner, Joseph, ed., *The Philosophy of John Dewey* (Henry Holt and Company, 1928).

Rauch, Jonathan, *Kindly Inquisitors: The New Attacks on Free Thought* (The University of Chicago Press, 1992).

Redish, Martin H., *Freedom of Expression: A Critical Analysis* (The Michie Company, 1984).

Revel, Jean-François, *Democracy against Itself: The Future of the Democratic Impulse* (Roger Kaplan, trans., The Free Press, 1993).

Rorty, Richard, *Consequences of Pragmatism* (University of Minnesota Press, 1982).

————, *Contingency, Irony and Solidarity* (Cambridge University Press, 1989).

————, *Essays on Heidegger and Others* (Cambridge University Press, 1991).

————, *Feminism and Pragmatism*, 30 Mich. Q. Rev. 231 (1991).

————, *Objectivity, Relativism, and Truth* (Cambridge University Press, 1991).

————, *Philosophy and the Mirror of Nature* (Princeton University Press, 1979).

Rosen, Jeffrey, *Fast Food Justice*, N.Y. Times, Nov. 16, 1993, at A27.

Rosenberg, D., *Racist Speech, the First Amendment, and Public Universities: Taking a Stand on Neutrality*, 76 Cornell L. Rev. 549, (1991).

Scholem, G., *On the Kabbalah & Its Symbolism* (Schocken Books, 1965).

Schumpeter, Joseph, *Capitalism, Socialism, and Democracy* (Harper & Row, 3d ed. 1975).

Searle, John, *The Battle over the University*, N.Y. Rev. of Books Dec. 6, 1990, at 34.

Simon, John, *Odd Couples*, 42 National Review, Dec. 31, 1990, at 46.

Siskind, Lawrence J., *The Folly and Futility of Censoring Violence*, Legal Times, Nov. 22, 1993, at 28.

Smolla, Rodney A., *Free Speech and Religious, Racial and Sexual Harassment*, 32 Wm. & Mary L. Rev. 207 (1991).

———, *Free Speech in an Open Society* (Alfred A. Knopf, 1992).

Sowell, Thomas, *Ethnic America* (Basic Books, 1981).

Spinoza, Benedict, *Theological-Political Treatise, in* The Chief Works of Benedict Spinoza (R.H.M. Elwes, trans., G. Bell, 1883).

Stanley, Alessandra, *Hidden Hollywood*, N.Y. Times, May 31, 1992, § 9, at 1.

"The Storm over The University": An Exchange, N.Y. Rev. of Books, Feb. 14, 1991 at 48.

Strauss, Marcy, *Sexual Speech in the Workplace*, 25 Harv. C.R.-C.L. L. Rev. 1 (1990).

Strossen, Nadine, *Defending Pornography* (Scribner, 1995).

———, *Regulating Racist Speech on Campus: A Modest Proposal*, 1990 Duke L. J. 484.

Sunstein, Cass R., *Free Speech Now*, 59 U. Chi. L. Rev. 255 (1992).

———, *Low Value Speech Revisited*, 83 Nw. U. L. Rev. 555 (1989).

———, *Pornography and the First Amendment*, 1986 Duke L.J. 589.

Tierney, John, *Porn, the Low-Slung Engine of Progress*, N.Y. Times, Jan. 9, 1994, § 2, at 18.

Tower, John, *Consequences: A Personal and Political Memoir* (Little, Brown, 1991).

Tribe, Laurence H., *American Constitutional Law* (The Foundation Press, 2d ed. 1988).

Vines, Michael, *In Baptist Talk, Clinton Stresses Moral Themes*, N.Y. Times, Sept. 10, 1994, at A1.

Volokh, Eugene, *Freedom of Speech and Workplace Harassment*, 39 UCLA L. Rev. 1791 (1992).

West, Robin, *The Feminist-Conservative Anti-Pornography Alliance and the 1986 Attorney General's Commission on Pornography Report*, 1987 Am. B. Found. Res. J. 681 (1987).

Wilford, John N., *"Venus" Figurines from Ice Age Rediscovered in an Antique Shop*, N.Y. Times, Feb. 1, 1994, at C11.

Wilson, A.N., *Biography of C.S. Lewis* (Norton, 1st American ed. 1990).

Winter, Ralph K., *A First Amendment Overview*, 55 Brooklyn L. Rev. 71 (1989).

Wittgenstein, Ludwig, *On Certainty* (G.E.M. Anscome and G.H. von Wright, eds., Harper & Row, 1969).

Wolfson, Nicholas, *Corporate First Amendment Rights and the SEC* (Quorum Books, 1990).

INDEX

About the Author

NICHOLAS WOLFSON is the George and Helen England Professor of Law at the University of Connecticut School of Law where he teaches courses in Free Speech, Securities Regulation and Corporate Law. He has published extensively in these fields; his books include *Corporate First Amendment Rights and the SEC* (Quorum, 1990) and *The Modern Corporation: Free Markets vs. Regulation* (1984).